新双双中文教材 7
New Chinese Language and Culture Course

中国地理常识
Common Chinese Geography Textbook

王双双 编著

北京大学出版社
PEKING UNIVERSITY PRESS

NanHai
BRIDGING EAST & WEST

图书在版编目（CIP）数据

中国地理常识/王双双编著. —2版. —北京：北京大学出版社，2017.8（2022.1重印）
（新双双中文教材）
ISBN 978-7-301-28407-0

Ⅰ.①中… Ⅱ.①王… Ⅲ.①汉语—对外汉语教学—教材 ②地理—中国 Ⅳ.①H195.4

中国版本图书馆CIP数据核字（2017）第133190号

书中地图插图由中国地图出版社授权使用。
审图号：GS（2017）2401号

书　　　　名	中国地理常识（第二版） ZHONGGUO DILI CHANGSHI
著作责任者	王双双　编著
英文翻译	[德] Nanny Kim（金兰中）
责任编辑	邓晓霞
标 准 书 号	ISBN 978-7-301-28407-0
出版发行	北京大学出版社
地　　　　址	北京市海淀区成府路205号　100871
网　　　　址	http://www.pup.cn　　　新浪微博：@北京大学出版社
电子信箱	zpup@pup.cn
电　　　　话	邮购部 62752015　发行部 62750672　编辑部 62767349
印 刷 者	三河市博文印刷有限公司
经 销 者	新华书店
	889毫米×1194毫米　16开本　12.25印张　110千字
	2006年7月第1版
	2017年8月第2版　2022年3月第4次印刷
定　　　　价	80.00元（含课本、练习本、手工作业）

未经许可，不得以任何方式复制或抄袭本书之部分或全部内容。
版权所有，侵权必究
举报电话：010-62752024　电子信箱：fd@pup.pku.edu.cn
图书如有印装质量问题，请与出版部联系，电话：010-62756370

第二版序

能够与北京大学出版社合作出版"双双中文教材"的第二版,让这套优秀的对外汉语教材泽被更多的学生,加州中文教学研究中心备感荣幸。

这是一套洋溢着浓浓爱意的教材。作者的女儿在美国出生,到了识字年龄,作者教她学习过市面上流行的多套中文教材,但都强烈地感觉到这些教材"水土不服"。一解女儿学习中文的燃眉之急,是作者编写这套教材的初衷和原动力。为了让没有中文环境的孩子能够喜欢学习中文,作者字斟句酌地编写课文;为了赋予孩子审美享受、引起他们的共鸣,作者特邀善画儿童创作了一幅幅稚气可爱的插图;为了加深孩子们对内容的理解,激发孩子们的学习热情,作者精心设计了充满创造性的互动活动。

这是一套承载着文化传承使命感的教材。语言不仅仅是文化的载体,更是文化重要的有机组成部分。学习一门外语的深层障碍往往根植于目标语言与母语间的文化差异。这种差异对于学习中文的西方学生尤为突出。这套教材的使用对象正处在好奇心和好胜心最强的年龄阶段,作者抓住了这一特点,变阻力为动力,一改过去削学生认知能力和智力水平之"足"以适词汇和语言知识之"履"的通病。教材在高年级部分,一个学期一个文化主题,以对博大精深的中国文化的探索激发学生的学习兴趣,使学生在学习语言的同时了解璀璨的中国文化。

"双双中文教材"自2005年面世以来,受到了老师、学生和家长的广泛欢迎。很多觉得中文学习枯燥无味而放弃的学生,因这套教材发现了学习中文的乐趣,又重新回到了中文课堂。本次修订,作者不仅吸纳了老师们对于初版的反馈意见和自己实际使用过程中的心得,还参考了近年对外汉语教学理论及实践方面的成果。语言学习部分由原来的九册改为五册,一学年学习一册,文化学习部分保持一个专题一册。相信修订后的"新双双中文教材"会更方便、实用,让更多学生受益。

张晓江
美国加州中文教学研究中心秘书长

第一版前言

"双双中文教材"是一套专门为海外青少年编写的中文课本，是我在美国八年的中文教学实践基础上编写成的。在介绍这套教材之前，请读一首小诗：

> 一双神奇的手，
> 推开一扇窗。
> 一条神奇的路，
> 通向灿烂的中华文化。

鲍凯文　鲍维江

鲍维江和鲍凯文姐弟俩是美国生美国长的孩子，也是我的学生。1998年冬，他们送给我的新年贺卡上的小诗，深深地打动了我的心。我把这首诗看成我文化教学的"回声"。我要传达给海外每位中文老师：我教给他们（学生）中国文化，他们思考了、接受了、回应了。这条路走通了！

语言是一种交流的工具，更是一种文化和一种生活方式，所以学习中文也就离不开中华文化的学习。汉字是一种古老的象形文字，她从远古走来，带有大量的文化信息，但学起来并不容易。使学生增强兴趣、减小难度，走出苦学汉字的怪圈，走进领悟中华文化的花园，是我编写这套教材的初衷。

学生不论大小，天生都有求知的欲望，都有欣赏文化美的追求。中华文化本身是魅力十足的。把这宏大而玄妙的文化，深入浅出地，有声有色地介绍出来，让这迷人的文化如涓涓细流，一点一滴地渗入学生们的心田，使学生们逐步体味中国文化，是我编写这套教材的目的。

为此我将汉字的学习放入文化介绍的流程之中同步进行，让同学们在学中国地理的同时，学习汉字；在学中国历史的同时，学习汉字；在学中国哲学的同时，学习汉字；在学中国科普文选的同时，学习汉字……

这样的一种中文学习，知识性强，趣味性强；老师易教，学生易学。当学生们合上书本时，他们的眼前是中国的大好河山，是中国五千年的历史和妙不可言的哲学思维，是奔腾的现代中国……

总之，他们了解了中华文化，就会探索这片土地，热爱这片土地，就会与中国结下情缘。

最后我要衷心地感谢所有热情支持和帮助我编写教材的老师、家长、学生、朋友和家人。特别是老同学唐玲教授、何茜老师和我女儿Uta Guo年复一年的鼎力相助。可以说这套教材是大家努力的结果。

王双双

课程设置（建议）

序号	书名	适用年级
1	中文课本　第一册	幼儿园/一年级
2	中文课本　第二册	二年级
3	中文课本　第三册	三年级
4	中文课本　第四册	四年级
5	中文课本　第五册	五年级
6	中国成语故事	六年级
7	中国地理常识	六年级
8	中国古代故事	七年级
9	中国神话传说	七年级
10	中国古代科学技术	八年级
11	中国民俗与民间艺术	八年级
12	中国文学欣赏	九年级
13	中国诗歌欣赏	九年级
14	中国古代哲学	十年级
15	中国历史	十年级

目录

第一课	亚洲最大的国家	1
第二课	人口和民族	7
第三课	山地和高原	14
第四课	平原和盆地	21
第五课	江河与湖泊	27
第六课	气候	35
第七课	农作物和名产	44
第八课	野生动植物	50
第九课	行政区划	56
第十课	著名城市	62
第十一课	中国名山（选修课）	71
第十二课	名胜古迹（选修课）	76
生字表（简）		82
生字表（繁）		84
生词表（简）		86
生词表（繁）		88
附录	"新双双中文教材"写作练习（1—7册）	90
附录	中国政区图	91
附录	中国地形图	92

第一课
亚洲最大的国家

中国位于地球的北半球,亚洲的东部,太平洋的西岸。

中国领土广阔,陆地面积960万平方千米,和欧洲几乎相等,是亚洲最大的国家。

中国的陆上邻国有朝鲜、俄罗斯、蒙古、巴基斯坦、印度、尼泊尔、缅甸和越南等14个国家。与中国隔海相望的国家,东面是韩国、日本,南面是菲律宾等国。

中国的海岸线很长,从北向南有渤海、黄海、东海和南海,海上大小岛屿有5,000多个。

生词

yà zhōu 亚洲	Asia	miàn jī 面积	area
wèi yú 位于	locate	píng fāng 平方	square
dì qiú 地球	earth	ōu zhōu 欧洲	Europe
dōng bù 东部	east	měng gǔ 蒙古	Mongolia
tài píng yáng 太平洋	the Pacific Ocean	yìn dù 印度	India
xī àn 西岸	west coast	gé hǎi xiāng wàng 隔海相望	adjacent across the sea
lǐng tǔ 领土	territory	hǎi àn xiàn 海岸线	coastline
guǎng kuò 广阔	vast	dǎo yǔ 岛屿	islands
lù dì 陆地	continent		

选学生词

cháo xiǎn 朝鲜	the Democratic People's Republic of Korea	yuè nán 越南	Vietnam
é luó sī 俄罗斯	Russia	hán guó 韩国	the Republic of Korea
ní bó ěr 尼泊尔	Nepal	rì běn 日本	Japan
miǎn diàn 缅甸	Burma	fēi lǜ bīn 菲律宾	the Philippines
		bó hǎi 渤海	the Bohai Sea

听写

亚洲　　位于　　广阔　　面积　　岛屿　　蒙古

印度　　陆地　　太平洋　　*隔海相望　　领土

注：*号以后为选做题，后同。

词语运用

位于

① 中国位于亚洲的东部，太平洋的西岸。

② 法国位于欧洲的西部。

"岛"字的演变

 島 岛

看地图找出中国和欧洲（说出颜色）

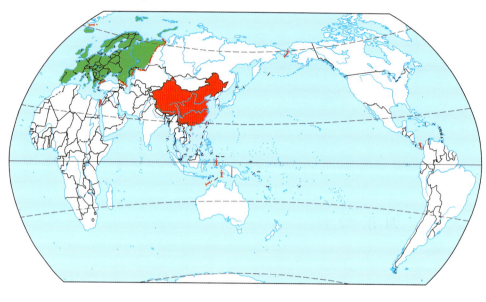

中国_____   欧洲_____

回答问题

1.中国的位置在哪里？

2.中国是亚洲最大的国家吗？

3.中国的邻国有多少个？请说出5个。

中国位置顺口溜

秋香提供

亚洲东，大洋西，
东西南北各五千。
北漠河，南海岛，
帕米尔，乌苏里。
广阔中国多美丽！

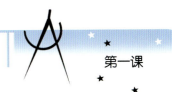

阅读

中 国

中国大地广阔美丽，南北长5,500千米。当北方的黑龙江还是冰天雪地的冬天，南海诸(zhū)岛已是鲜花开放。中国东西长5,000千米，时差(chā)4小时。当太阳从乌苏里江升起时，帕(pà)米尔高原还是星斗(dǒu)满天的夜晚。

诗歌

春天来了

春天来了，　春天来了！
海南岛上，　盛(shèng)开着鲜花；
长江两岸，　柳(liǔ)枝刚刚发芽(yá)；
长白山上，　还在飞舞雪花。
这就是中国，　辽(liáo)阔美丽的国家。

长白山树挂

海南岛

长江两岸

The Largest Country in Asia

China is on the northern hemisphere of our globe, in the eastern part of Asia and on the western shores of the Pacific.

The Chinese territory is vast, with its 9.6 million square kilometres, it is almost the same size as Europe and it is the largest country in Asia.

China has land borders with 14 countries. Among these are North Korea, Russia, Mongolia, Pakistan, India, Nepal, Burma and Vietnam. Neighbors across the sea are South Korea in the east and, Japan, the Philippines in the south.

China's long coast extends from the Bohai Sea, to the Yellow Sea, the East China Sea and the South China Sea, with some 5000 islands large and small.

China

China is a vast and beautiful country. From north to south, it extends over 5500 km. When Heilongjiang is still under ice and snow, the flowers are in full bloom on the islands of the South China Sea. China extends over 5000 km from east to west and the time difference is four hours. When the sun rises over the Wusuli River, the Pamir Mountains still sleep under the stars.

Spring Is Here

Spring is here, yes spring is here!
Fragrant flowers abound on Hainan Island,
The willows are budding on the banks of the Changjiang,
While snowflakes still swirl on the Changbai Mountains.
This is China, a vast and beautiful country.

第二课
人口和民族

中国是世界上人口最多的国家，近14亿人，占世界人口的19%。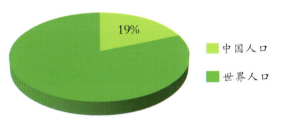中国虽然人口多，但分布很不平均，90%的人居住在东部；占全国土地一半的西部地区，人口只占10%。

在中国广阔的土地上，居住着56个民族。汉族人口最多，占全国人口的91%，其他55个少数民族的人口有1亿多，其中主要有壮族、蒙古族、回族、维吾尔族、藏族、满族等。少数民族主要居住在中国的西南、西北和东北地区。

现在，中国人的平均寿命为76岁。儿童可以免费上小学和*中学。大学生的人数也在上升。

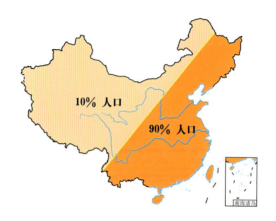

生词

rén kǒu 人口	population	hàn zú 汉族	Han nationality
mín zú 民族	nationality	qí tā 其他	other
shì jiè 世界	world	wéi wú ěr zú 维吾尔族	Uygur nationality
yì 亿	a hundred million	zàng zú 藏族	Tibetan nationality
zhàn 占	account for	dì qū 地区	region
fēn bù 分布	distribute	shòu mìng 寿命	life-span
píng jūn 平均	average	miǎn fèi 免费	free
jū zhù 居住	reside		

---

*中学：这里指初中。

听写

民族　世界　分布　平均　汉族　其他　地区

居住　免费　*亿　寿命

词语运用

免费

① 这是免费的报纸。

② 今晚，学校有免费的电影。

③ 机场有免费的交通车。

平均

① 我校游泳队的平均年龄为12岁。

② 他们班数学考试平均分为86分。

回答问题

1. 中国有多少人口？讲讲中国人口的分布。

2. 中国有多少个民族？主要有哪xiē些民族？

3. 你自己是哪个民族的？

阅读

民族节日

一、那达慕

"那达慕"大会是蒙古族的重要活动，也是重要的节日。每年的七八月，内蒙古草原百花开放，大草原上举行"那达慕"大会，主要活动是骑马、射箭和摔跤比赛。蒙古族的小朋友五六岁就开始参加这些比赛。

赛马比赛

射箭比赛

摔跤比赛

二、开斋节

开斋节是回族的主要节日。过节时，回族人穿上干净的衣服，到清真寺参加会礼。家家户户都做好吃的油香。维吾尔族等很多少数民族也过开斋节。

开斋节

三、泼水节

泼水节是傣族的节日。时间在清明前后，要过三天。每到泼水节，人们相互泼水，唱歌、跳舞、赛龙船，十分热闹。

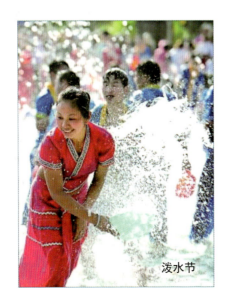
泼水节

中国地理常识

阅读生词

nà dá mù
那达慕　Naadam

shuāi jiāo
摔跤　wrestling

bǐ sài
比赛　match, games

qīng zhēn sì
清真寺　mosque

pō shuǐ jié
泼水节　Water Sprinkling Festival

歌曲

五十六个民族

五十六个民族，五十六朵花。

五十六个民族是一家。

五十六个民族，五十六朵花。

爱我中华，爱我中华，爱我中华！

孔令乔（8岁）　画

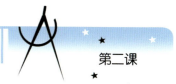

第二课

The Population and the Nationalities

China is the country with the largest population on earth; approaching 1.4 billion people, or 19% of humanity. This large population is distributed very unevenly. 90% live in eastern China, while western China occupies half of the country but only 10% of the population lives here.

The extensive territories of China are home to 56 nationalities. The Han nationality is the largest, making up for 91% of the population. Some 100 million people belong to the other 55 nationalities. The largest of these are the Zhuang, the Mongols, the Hui, the Uygurs, the Tibetans, and the Manchus.*Most minorities live in the Southwest, the Northwest and the Northeast.

At present, the average life expectancy in China is 76 years. Children enjoy free primary and middle schools. The number of university students is rising.

Minority Festivals

1 The Naadam Festival

The Naadam Convention is an important Mongolian event and a great festival. It is held in July or August, when the flowers blossom on the grasslands. The main activities are horse racing, archery and wrestling. Mongolian children begin to take part when they are only five or six years old.

2 The Eid al-Fitr or the Sugar Feast

The Sugar Feast is the highest Muslim holiday. Everyone puts on clean clothes and goes to the mosque for a service. Each and every family prepares tasty fried pasties. The Muslim minorities in China, such as the Hui and the Uygurs, also celebrate Eid al-Fitr.

3 The Water Sprinkling or Songkran Festival

The Water Sprinkling Festival is the Dai/Thai New-Year festival. It is held in early spring and lasts for three days. On this festival, everybody throws water at everybody else, there is singing, dancing, dragon boat races, and a lot of excitement.

---

* Ranked by population, the nine largest minorities are the Zhuang (16.9 million), the Uyghurs (11.5 million), the Hui (10.5 million), the Manchu (10.3 million), the Miao (9.4 million), the Yi (8.7 million), the Tujia (8.3 million), the Tibetans (6.2 million), and the Mongols (5.9 million).

第三课
山地和高原

中国是一个多山的国家,山地和高原占全国面积的2/3,地势西高东低,像阶梯一样。

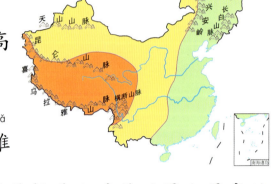

中国主要的山脉有喜马拉雅山、昆仑山、天山和横断山等。喜马拉雅山脉是世界上最高的山脉(主峰珠穆朗玛峰海拔8,844.43米,是世界第一高峰)。

中国的高原主要在中西部。

第一阶梯是青藏高原,平均海拔在4,000米以上。那里高

寒，湖泊多，有许多高大的雪山。

第二阶梯是内蒙古高原、黄土高原和云贵高原，平均海拔在1,000—2,000米之间。内蒙古高原的许多地方，是水草肥美的草原。那儿牛羊成群，马儿奔跑，云雀歌唱。黄土高原，地表为厚厚的黄土层。云贵高原，地面高低不平，是个多山的高原。

第三阶梯在中国的东部，海拔多在500米以下。这里是平原地区。

青藏高原　　　　　　　　　　　内蒙古高原
黄土高原　　　　　　　　　　　云贵高原

生词

gāo yuán 高原	plateau	gāo hán 高寒	high and frigid
dì shì 地势	terrain	hú pō 湖泊	lake
jiē tī 阶梯	ladder	nèi měng gǔ 内蒙古	Inner Mongolia
shān mài 山脉	mountain range	féi měi 肥美	lush
kūn lún shān 昆仑山	the Kunlun Mountains	tǔ céng 土层	layer of soil
héng duàn shān 横断山	the Hengduan Mountains	píng yuán 平原	plain
hǎi bá 海拔	elevation		

听写

高原　　地势　　高寒　　湖泊　　山脉　　海拔　　肥美

土层　　平原　　*横断山

词语运用

海拔

① 青藏高原的平均海拔在4,000米以上。

② 布达拉宫建在海拔3,700米的高山上。

③ 这座山海拔1,000米。

回答问题

1. 讲一讲中国地势的特点。

2. 说出中国主要的几条山脉。

3. 说出中国的四大高原。

阅读

布达(dá)宫(gōng)

世界上最高的宫殿(diàn)，是西藏(sà)拉萨的布达拉宫。她建在海拔3,700米的山上，已有1,300年的历史了。布达拉宫高13层，直入蓝天。顺台阶一步步往上走，好像来到天宫。

拉萨布达拉宫

宫殿有2,000多个房间，宫内有壁(bì)画、佛经等历史文物。布达拉宫是藏民族的文化中心。

离太阳最近的地方

离太阳最近的地方

——中国西藏。

雪山上的宫殿

——金碧(bì)辉(huī)煌(huáng)。

那是布达拉宫，布达拉宫！

——拉萨，西藏！

牦牛——高原之舟

捡牛粪

骑牦牛巡逻

牦牛生活在青藏高原上。它的毛又多又长，像穿了一件厚厚的大衣。牦牛能在冰天雪地里过冬，还可以背很重的东西爬山、过冰河，是高原上的"车"和"船"，被称为"高原之舟"。藏民喝牦牛奶，吃牦牛肉，用它的毛做衣服和帐篷，连做饭、取暖都烧干牦牛粪。真可以说牦牛全身都是宝，藏民的生活离不开牦牛。

牦牛运货

牛粪是财富的象征

Mountains and Highlands

China is mountainous: two thirds of the territory are mountains and highlands. Overall, the land descends from the west to the east.

The main mountains are the Himalayas, the Kunlun Mountains, the Tianshan and the Hengduan Mountains. The Himalayas are the highest mountains in the world (with the highest peak, Mount Everest towering at 8,844.43 m).

The central western part of China mainly consists of highlands.

You can imagine three giant steps descending towards the sea:

The highest step is the Tibet-Qinghai Plateau, on average over 4,000 m above the sea level. It is cold, with many lakes and great snow-covered peaks.

The second step is the Mongolian Plateau, the Loess Plateau, and the Yunnan-Guizhou Plateau, with the altitudes mostly between 1,000 and 2,000 m. On the Mongolian Plateau, there are many places with lush grasslands, where cattle and sheep form large flocks and horses run freely, while the birds sing in the sky. There are even wild cattle that can run long distances. The Loess Plateau consists of thick layers of yellow earth. The Yunnan and Guizhou Plateau is covered with rugged landscape mountain peaks.

The third step is Eastern China. Most of the land here is under 500 m; this is the region of the great plains.

The Potala Palace

The highest palace on earth is the Potala Palace in Tibet. It is built on a mountain that is 3,700 m above the sea level, and has a history of 1,300 years. The Potala Palace with its 13 stories seems to climb straight into the blue sky. When you climb the stairs, it feels like entering a palace of heaven.

The palace with its over 2,000 rooms, murals, sutras and cultural relics is the cultural centre of the Tibetan people.

Yaks: The Boats of the Tibetan Plateau

Yaks live on the Tibet-Qinghai Plateau. They have extremely dense and long fur like an extra thick overcoat. They don't mind the icy cold winter, and can carry heavy loads up the mountains and across icy rivers. They are the "carts" or "boats" of the highlands. The Tibetans drink their milk, eat their meat, make clothes and tents from their hides and furs, and cook meals by burning their dung. Everything the yak produces is valuable, Tibetan life is inconceivable without them.

第四课
平原和盆地

中国的平原主要在东部，占全国面积的19%。中国的三大平原是东北平原、华北平原、长江中下游平原。

东北平原是中国最大的平原，肥沃的黑土地一望无边。夏日，麦浪滚滚像金色的海洋。

华北平原位于北京、天津、河北、河南、山东等地。

长江中下游平原在湖北、江苏、浙江、上海等地。这里，人口稠密，经济发达，是中国的鱼米之乡。

中国有四大盆地：塔里木盆地、柴(chái)达(dá)木盆地、准噶(gá)尔盆地和四川盆地。这四大盆地都在中国的西部。

塔里木盆地位于天山以南，这里有中国最大的沙漠——塔克拉玛干沙漠。

准噶尔盆地位于天山以北，北冰洋的湿润空气可以进入盆地内，所以降水较多，是古代通往中亚的通道。

四川盆地位于四川东部，这里气候湿润，农业发达。

中国地理常识

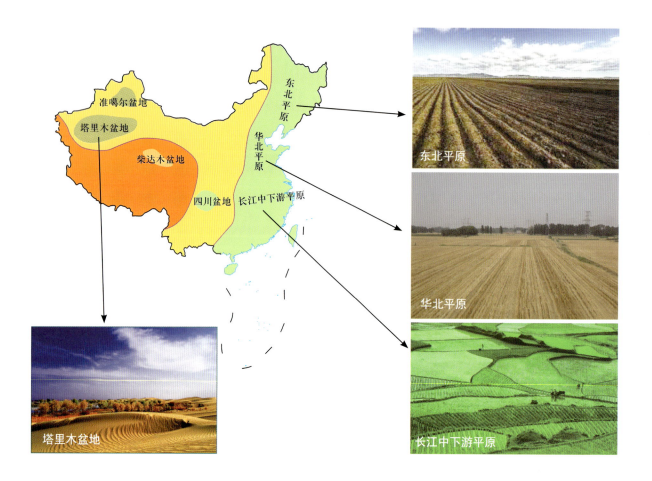

生词

pén dì 盆地	basin	jiàng shuǐ 降水	rainfall
féi wò 肥沃	fertile	nèi 内	inside, in
tiān jīn 天津	Tianjin	tōng dào 通道	channel
zhè jiāng 浙江	Zhejiang (Province)	qì hòu 气候	climate
chóu mì 稠密	dense	shī rùn 湿润	humid
jīng jì 经济	economy	nóng yè 农业	agriculture
fā dá 发达	developed		

选学生词

tǎ kè lā mǎ gān shā mò
塔克拉玛干沙漠　　the Taklamakan Desert

zhǔn gá ěr pén dì
准噶尔盆地　　the Junggar Basin

听写

盆地　浙江　经济　发达　降水　通道　内

气候　湿润　农业　*稠密

比一比

经 { 经过 / 经济 }　　达 { 发达 / 达到 }　　通 { 通知 / 通道 }

反义词

内——外　　　　发达——落后

23

词语运用

经济

① 上海经济正在飞快地发展。

② 中国的中西部经济不太发达。

发达

① 美国是发达国家。

② 上海的经济很发达。

③ 法国的绘画艺术很发达。

回答问题

1. 中国有哪些大平原？请在地图上找出。

2. 中国有哪些大盆地？请在地图上找出。

阅读

最长的沙漠公路

塔里木沙漠公路，是世界上流动沙漠中最长的公路。它穿过塔里木盆地，全长525千米。公路两边有水井，种植了2,000万棵植物，成了沙漠中的绿色走廊(láng)。

塔里木沙漠公路

万丈盐桥

柴达木盆地有一座神奇的长桥，在察尔汗盐湖上。桥不用水泥，不用钢铁(gāng tiě)，不用木头，而是用盐铺(pū)成的"万丈盐桥"。这是一种难得一见的路桥。公路就像一座桥浮(fú)在湖面上，全长32千米，将盐湖从中间分成两半，是柴达木盆地的一大奇观。

万丈盐桥

The Plains and the Basins

The plains are in the east and account for 19% of China's land surface. There are three great plains, the Northeast China Plain, the North China Plain, and the Middle-Lower Changjiang Plain.

The Northeast China Plain is the largest, rich black soil extends further than the eye can see. In summer, when the wheat ripens, it looks like a golden sea.

Beijing, Tianjin, Hebei, Henan and Shandong are located in the North China Plain.

Along Middle and Lower Yangtze River are the provinces of Hubei, Jiangsu, Zhejiang and Shanghai. This region is densely populated and economically strong. It is the land of rice and fish.

China has four great basins: the Tarim Basin, the Qaidam Basin, the Junggar Basin, and the Sichuan Basin. All of these are in Western China.

The Tarim Basin is to the south of the Tianshan Mountains, here is the Taklamakan—China's largest desert.

The Junggar Basin is to north of the Tianshan. From the north, moist air from the Arctic Ocean enters this basin, therefore it is comparatively humid. The ancient road linking across Central Asia led through this basin.

The Sichuan Basin is in the east of Sichuan Province. It enjoys a humid climate and has a highly developed agriculture.

The Longest Desert Road

The Tarim Desert Highway is the longest road on earth across shifting sand dunes. For a total of 525 km, it runs through the Tarim Basin. There are wells on both sides of the road and 20 million trees were planted, so that it became a green corridor across the desert.

The Salt Bridge

There is a bridge on Qarhan Salt Lake in the Qaidam Basin. The bridge was not built from concrete, steel or timber, but from salt cakes! The Salt Bridge is a unique bridge in the world. It seems to float on the lake; in fact, it runs on a dike built from salt, which is 32 km long and divides the lake into two parts. It is one of the spectaculars of the Qaidam Basin.

第五课
江河与湖泊

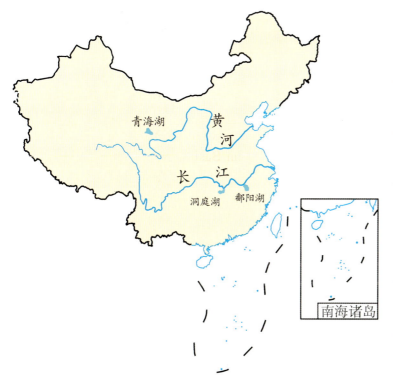

中国有许多大江大河,主要有长江、黄河、黑龙江、珠江等。其中最著名的是黄河和长江。

黄河和长江都发源于青藏高原,自西向东流入大海。黄河位于中国北部,全长5,464千米,是中国的第二大河。它流经黄土地区,带着大量黄土泥沙,所以称黄河。黄河是中国古代文明的发源地,被称为母亲河。

长江,中国第一大河,全长6,300千米,是一条名副其实的"长河",也是世界第三大河。长江流域是中国经济最繁荣的地区,重要城市有重庆、武汉、南京、上海。长江水资源丰富,还是中国内河航运的"黄金水道"。

黄河

长江

中国的湖泊很多。最大的淡水湖是鄱(pó)阳湖（江西），第二大淡水湖是洞庭湖（湖南），最大的咸水湖是青海湖（青海）。鄱阳湖水量变化大，像是长江的水库。这里也是鸟的天堂，有300多种鸟生活。成千上万只候鸟到这里过冬，其中白鹤(hè)最多。

鄱阳湖国家湿地公园

生词

cháng jiāng 长江	the Changjiang River	liú yù 流域	river basin
huáng hé 黄河	the Yellow River	fán róng 繁荣	prosperous, glory
fā yuán 发源	originate	háng yùn 航运	shipping
liú jīng 流经	flow through	fēng fù 丰富	abundant
wén míng 文明	civilization	zī yuán 资源	resource
chēng wéi 称为	be known as	shuǐ kù 水库	reservoir
míng fù qí shí 名副其实	worthy of the name		

听写

发源　流经　文明　称为　流域　繁荣　航运

丰富　资源　*名副其实

比一比

原

原 { 平原
　　 高原

源

源 { 发源
　　 资源

词语运用

原

① 中国最大的平原是东北平原。

② 近年来，农民们在黄土高原上种了许多苹果树。

源

① 黄河是中国古代文明的发源地。

② 黄河和长江都发源于青藏高原。

③ 长江水力资源丰富。

名副其实

① 姚明是名副其实的篮球巨人。

② 手机是我们名副其实的好助手。

③ 长江全长6,300千米，是一条名副其实的"长河"。

回答问题

1. 黄河在中国南方还是北方？是中国的第几大河？

2. 长江是世界第几大河？

3. 中国的主要湖泊有哪几个？

阅读

黄河的"地上河"

黄河发源于青藏高原，流过黄土高原时，带入大量泥沙，有"一碗水，半碗泥"的说法，是世界上泥沙最多的河流。

黄河禹门

当黄河冲出禹门进入下游，河道变宽，水流变慢，泥沙沉在河床中，慢慢河道高出两岸平地，成了著名的"地上河"，要修建堤(dī)坝(bà)挡水。不少河段高出地面10米。因此黄河常发生水灾和改道。现在人们在黄土高原种树、种草，减少黄土流失。

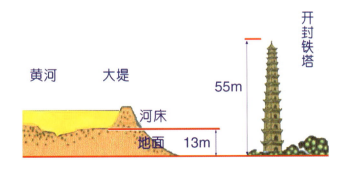

黄河禹门

黄土高原上的苹果园

问题

1. 想一想，如何治理黄河，让黄河水变清？

歌曲

龙的传人 [节选]

遥(yáo)远的东方有一条江,

她的名字叫长江。

遥远的东方有一条河,

她的名字叫黄河。

古老的东方有一条龙,

她的名字叫中国。

黑眼睛,黑头发,黄皮肤,

永永远远是龙的传人。

阮思齐(12岁) 画

Rivers and Lakes

There are some major rivers of China: the Changjiang, the Huanghe, the Heilongjiang, and the Zhujiang. The Huanghe and the Changjiang are the most famous rivers among them.

These two rivers originate to the far west in the Tibet-Qinghai Plateau, from where they flow eastwards and eventually into the sea. The Huanghe is 5,464 km long; it is the second largest river of China. It flows through the loess region, and its waters take a lot of yellow soil with them, for this reason it is called the Yellow River. The ancient civilization of China originated on the banks of this river, which is therefore, called "the mother river."

The Chanjiang with a total length of over 6,300 km, is the longest river of China, truly fitting its name "Long River". It is the third longest river on earth. The regions drained by the Changjiang are the most flourishing areas of China, with many important cities, such as Chongqing, Wuhan, Nanjing, and Shanghai. The large water body is also a shipping artery of key importance.

Lakes are very numerous in China. The largest fresh water lake is the Poyang Lake (in Jiangxi), the second one is Dongting Lake (in Hunan), while Qinghai Lake (in Qinghai) is the largest salt water lake. The water level of Poyang Lake fluctuates dramatically in different seasons, it serves as a reservoir to the Changjiang. It is also a bird paradise, inhabited by over 300 bird species. Huge flocks of migratory birds spend the winter here, of which the snow crane is the most.

The Huanghe, A River Running "above the Land"

The Huanghe originates in the Tibet-Qinghai Plateau: On it's long course through the Loess Plateaus, the river picks up much yellow earth. There is a saying that goes "One bowl of water contains half a bowl of mud." It has the highest sediment concentration of any river in the world.

After passing through Yumen, the Huanghe reaches its lower course, where it slows down and meanders. In these sluggish waters, a lot of sediment is deposited in the channel, and this means that the river bed rises until it is higher than the surrounding plain, and the river comes to run "above the land". It is contained by high dikes. In places, the river runs 10 m above the surrounding land. Therefore, the Huanghe has caused many disastrous floods when it changed its course. Now people plant trees and grass on the Loess Plateaus to reduce erosion.

第六课
气　候

中国领土广阔，气候也复杂多样，主要有三个特点：东部的季风气候、北部的大陆性气候和西部青藏高原的高寒气候。

一、季风气候

中国位于欧亚大陆，面对太平洋，受大陆和海洋影响，东部是季风气候。冬季，冷风从大陆吹向海洋，中国大地寒冷，风大。夏季，中国普遍炎热，海洋季风吹向大陆，带来大量雨水，因此降雨集中在夏季，气候是湿热多雨。这种"雨热同时"，对农业非常有利。

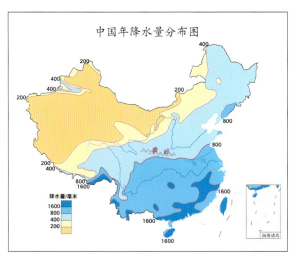

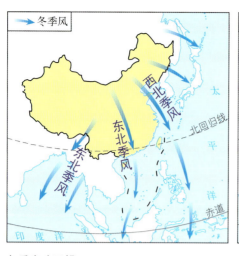
冬季寒冷干燥

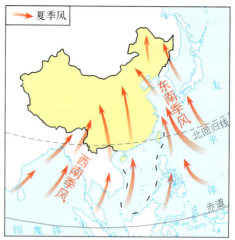
夏季炎热多雨

二、大陆性气候

中国的北部是大陆性气候。那里温差大，冬季，寒冷干燥；夏季，海洋季风吹不到那儿，因此炎热少雨。与地球同一纬度地带相比，中国是冬冷夏热。一月份，中国东北比法国温度低20℃；夏季七月份又比法国高4℃。

三、西部的高寒气候

中国西部的青藏高原，平均海拔4,000米以上，很多地方气温常年低于0℃，属于高寒气候。

另外，中国从北到南5,500千米，东北地区冬季长夏季短，而广东、台湾和海南四季常绿，几乎没有冬天。其他大部分地区四季分明。

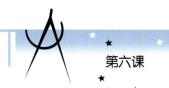

地点	纬度	1月平均气温	7月平均气温	气温年较差
齐齐哈尔	北纬47°23′	−19.6	22.6	42.2
巴黎	北纬48°58′	3.1	19.0	15.9
北京	北纬39°54′	−4.5	26.4	30.9
纽约	北纬40°40′	−0.8	22.8	23.6

生词

fù zá 复杂	complicated	jiàng yǔ 降雨	rainfall
tè diǎn 特点	characteristics	jí zhōng 集中	concentrate
jì fēng 季风	monsoon	wēn chā 温差	difference in temperature
pǔ biàn 普遍	common	gān zào 干燥	dry
yǐng xiǎng 影响	impact	wěi dù 纬度	latitude
yán rè 炎热	hot	fǎ guó 法国	France
yīn cǐ 因此	therefore, thus	shǔ yú 属于	belong to

听写

复杂　特点　季风　影响　炎热　因此　降雨

温差　干燥　属于　*集中　普遍

比一比

复 { 复杂 / 复习

夏 { 夏天 / 夏季

反义词

复杂——简单　　冷——炎热　　干燥——湿润

词语运用

复杂

① 中国气候复杂多样。

② 这个问题太复杂，我回答不了！

③ 事情不复杂，很简单。

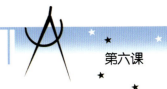

普遍

① 这里的学生普遍喜欢游泳。

② 夏季,中国普遍炎热。

③ 在中国,手机很普遍。

因此

① 夏天,季风从海洋吹向中国大陆,因此雨水多。

② 中国领土广阔,地势高低不同,因此气候多样。

回答问题

1. 中国降水最多的季节是哪个?

2. 在地图上找出法国巴黎与中国齐齐哈尔的纬度。

3. 什么是季风?(选做题)

4. 中国古诗中有"春风不度玉门关"的诗句,请在地图上找出玉门关,想想为什么春风吹不到那里。(选做题)

凉州词（zhōu）

王之涣（huàn）（唐代）

黄河远上白云间,一片孤城万仞山。（rèn）

羌笛何须怨杨柳,春风不度玉门关。（qiāng　xū yuànyáng liǔ）

中国地理常识

阅读

中国早在秦汉时已用二十四节气指导农业活动。

二十四节气歌

春雨惊春清谷天，

夏满芒夏暑相连，
（máng shǔ）

秋处露秋寒霜降，
（shuāng）

冬雪雪冬小大寒。

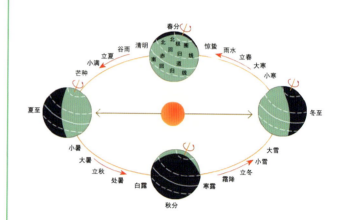

春天开始　　　降雨，不再降雪　　　土里的虫子惊醒了

日夜平分　　　踏青扫墓　　　五谷生长要雨水
　　　　　　　　　　　　　　春天过去了

阮思齐（12岁）　画

秦岭——中国南北分界线

中国中部的陕西省,有一条东西走向的大山——秦岭。它就像一面"挡风墙"挡住冬季的冷风不能南下,夏季的东南风不能北上。

秦岭东边的淮河是一条大河,秦岭和淮河就成了南方和北方的地理分界线。秦淮以北,河湖冬季结冰,树木多落叶;秦淮以南,河湖不结冰,树木不落叶,四季常绿。

秦岭很美,山林中有大熊猫、金丝猴等野生动物。秦岭历史厚重,千百年来在秦岭金牛道、陈仓道、荔枝道上留下了许多历史故事:金牛身后躲藏的士兵,"暗度陈仓"的大将军,身背荔枝骑马飞奔的信使……

古栈道

诸葛亮

秦岭古道图

Climate

Across the vast territory of China, climate is complex and varies greatly. Three main characteristics are: The monsoon in the east, the continental climate in the north, and the alpine climate of the Tibet-Qinghai Plateau in the west.

1) The monsoon climate

China is located on the Eurasian continent and faces the Pacific Ocean. Its climate is shaped by continental influence and by the ocean. In the east, the monsoon climate is dominant. In winter, cold air over the inland continental mass creates strong winds out to the sea. In summer, the air over the continent heats up and move from ocean towards land, which brings the monsoon rains. For this reason, rainfall is concentrated in the summer season and the weather is humid. The combination of rain and heat is particularly advantageous to agriculture.

2) The continental climate

The North of China has a continental climate, with pronounced temperature differences. Winters are dry and cold, while in summer the regions beyond the reach of the monsoon winds are baking hot yet rarely see rain. Compared to other places on the globe at the same altitude, Chinese winters are colder and the summers hotter. In January, the temperatures in the Chinese Northeast are 20℃ elsius lower than those of France, while they are 4℃ higher than those of France in July.

3) The alpine climate of the Tibet-Qinghai Plateau

The Tibet-Qinghai Plateau has an average elevation of over 4,000 m. In many places, temperatures are below 0℃ throughout the year. This is the zone of alpine climate.

Moreover, China extends over 5,500 km from north to south. In the Northeast, winters are long and summers short, while in Guangdong, Taiwan and Hainan, evergreen plants are lush through the year and there is hardly any winter. In many other parts, the four seasons are well-defined.

The 24 solar terms have been used to guide farming since the Qin and Han periods:

Song of Solar Terms

Early spring – life awakens – spring center – clear and bright – rain brings forth the grains.
Early summer – small harvest – grains ripen – midsummer – great heat joins.
Early autumn – heat withdrawds – cold arises – autumn center – ice forms and rawfrost falls.
Early winter – light snow – heavy snow – midwinter – light frost – severe frost.

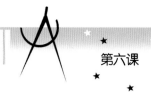

The Qinling Mountains: The Divide between the North and the South

In the middle of China in Shaanxi Province, there is a great mountain chain that runs east to west-the Qinling Mountains. The range forms a "windscreen" that stops the cold winds from entering the South in winter, and keep the east winds from the north in summer. East of the Qinling Mountains is the Qin-Huai line. This large river and the Qinling Mountains together form the dividing line between southern and northern China. North of the Qin-Huai line, rivers and lakes freeze in winter, and the trees lose their leaves; south of the Qin-Huai line, ice is practically unknown and many trees are evergreen.

The Qinling Mountains have a grand beauty, with pandas, gold silk monkeys and other wild animals in the mountain forests. They also have a long history. For times unknown, the golden ox road, the Chencang Road and the Litchi Road have crossed these mountains and left many stories: Soldiers that kept behind the golden ox; the general that secretly passed into Chencang; the messengers who carried Litchi branches while galloping past on their horses …

第七课
农作物和名产

中国是一个有着6,000年农业文明的国家。在这片土地上,物产丰富,主要农作物有水稻、小麦、棉花、谷子、大豆、黄麻等,其中水稻、大豆等起源于中国。

中国的水稻种植遍布全国,稻米产量占世界总产量的1/3。中国又是世界主要产棉国之一。棉区在黄河中下游、长江中下游地区和新疆地区。中国的棉花产量世界第一,占世界总产量的27%。

中国是最早发明养蚕取丝的国家,已有5,000年历史。中国丝绸之美闻名天下,被称为"丝绸之乡"。

谷子

稻子

麻

中国还是茶树的故乡。公元475年，中国茶已出口亚洲国家。中国的浙江、安徽、福建等省茶叶产量最大。中国茶品质上好，有绿茶、红茶、花茶等种类。

中国丝绸

生词

wù chǎn 物产	products	qǔ 取	get, take
nóng zuò wù 农作物	crops	wén míng tiān xià 闻名天下	famous
shuǐ dào 水稻	rice	gù xiāng 故乡	hometown
mián huā 棉花	cotton	gōng yuán 公元	Christian era
gǔ zi 谷子	millet	ān huī 安徽	Anhui (Province)
biàn bù 遍布	spread all over	fú jiàn 福建	Fujian (Province)
xīn jiāng 新疆	Xinjiang	pǐn zhì 品质	quality
chǎn liàng 产量	output	zhǒng lèi 种类	kind, species

中国地理常识

听写

水稻　　棉花　　谷子　　新疆　　棉花　　闻名　　福建

茶叶　　品质　　种类　　*遍布

词语运用

遍布

① 中国的水稻种植遍布全国。

② 通信网遍布全国。

③ 烤鸭店遍布北京。

品质

① 中国茶品质上好。

② 小华不但品质好，学习也很出色。

③ 在香港，服务品质真的不错。

回答问题

1. 中国主要的农作物有哪些？

2. 为什么中国被称为"丝绸之乡"？

3. 如果喝过中国茶，请说说茶的名字、颜色和味道(wèi)。

阅读

茶

中国有句话说:"开门七件事,柴米油盐酱(jiàng)醋(cù)茶。"可见人们生活中不可一日无茶。朋友来了一杯清茶相待,饭后一杯茶帮助消化。喝茶健康又让人心平气和,茶真是中国人的好朋友。

中国是茶的故乡,种茶、制(zhì)茶、饮(yǐn)茶都是最早的。传说是神农发现了茶可以喝,可以解毒(dú)。最早,中国人把茶作为药(yào)用,后来才成了家家户户的饮料(liào)。茶留香中国已有四五千年了。在中国云南、四川、安徽、浙江、福建等省都有大片的茶园。

中国茶种类很多,有绿茶、白茶、黄茶、红茶、乌龙茶、黑茶等。最著名的茶有:西湖龙井、信阳毛尖、铁(tiě)观音等。

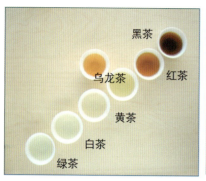

稻田养鱼

水稻种植在中国已有几千年历史了。稻田养鱼在中国青田也有700多年了。这是一种古老的农业种植系统，就是种稻时，在稻田里养鱼。鱼吃杂草和小虫，用身体翻动(tǎng)泥土和水，鱼粪(fèn)是水稻的肥料(liào)，真是又除草灭虫，又松土上肥。稻子熟了的时候，鱼也长大了。"千斤稻，百斤鱼"，鱼稻双丰收。

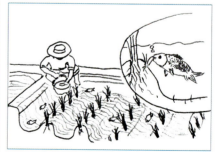

问题

请同学们查(chá)找一下，世界上还有哪些好的农业环(huán)保方法？

Agricultural Plants and Famous Products

Agricultural civilization in China goes back 6,000 years. Cultivation on Chinese soil is rich and varied, with rice, wheat, millet, cotton, soy beans, and hemp, while the domestication of rice and the soy bean originating in China.

Many varieties of rice are planted across the country, and 1/3 of the globally harvested rice is grown in Chinese fields. China is also one of the world's leading cotton producing countries. The main cotton growing areas are along the Lower Huanghe, the Middle and Lower Changjiang, and in Xinjiang. China is the leading producer of cotton, accounting for 27% of the global output.

The use of the thread of the silkworm was first discovered in China some 5,000 years ago. Chinese silk is renowned worldwide, and the county is known as the "home of silk."

China is also the home of tea cultivation. As early as 475 AD, we know of exports of the herb to other Asian countries. Tea plantations are most concentrated in Zhejiang, Anhui and Fujian. There are many varieties, such as green tea, black tea, and jasmine tea.

Tea

There is a saying in China: "You need seven things to set up home: firewood, rice, oil, salt, soy sauce, vinegar, and tea." This shows that people in China need tea every day of their life. When a friend visits, you need tea to offer; when you had a meal, you need it to have a digestion. Tea is good for your health, it keeps the mind clear and the temper even, a true friend of the Chinese people.

China is the home of tea, where the cultivation of the tea bush, the roasting of its leaves, and the art of brewing and drinking tea originated. Legend has it that Shennong found out that tea leaves could be used to make a drink and that it was an antidote against poison. At first, tea was used as medicine, and later on everyone in every household drank this beverage. The fragrance of tea has been known for some 4,000 years. Extensive tea plantations are found in Yunnan, Sichuan, Anhui, Zhejiang, and Fujian.

There are many tapes of tea, such as green tea, white tea, yellow tea, red tea, Oolong and black tea. The most famous teas are Longjing from the West Lake, Maojian from Xinyang, and Tieguanyin, the Iron Boddisatva.

Rice Paddies as Fish Ponds

Wet rice has been planted in China for several thousand years, and rice paddies have been used to breed fish for some 700 years. In this agricultural system, when rice is planted, fish are raised at the same time. The fish eat weeds and pests, while they stir the mud and the water, and their poo is a fertilizer for the rice. These fish help with weeding, pest control, loosening the soil and fertilizing. When the rice is ripe, the little fish have become big fish. "For 1000 pounds of rice, 100 pounds of fish can be harvested", a double harvest indeed.

第八课
野生动植物

白鳍豚

中国国土辽阔，自然条件复杂，是世界上野生动植物资源最丰富的国家之一。

中国有许多珍稀动物，如大熊猫、白鳍豚(qí tún)等。

大熊猫是人们喜爱的动物，它们只生长在中国四川、陕西和甘肃等地的几个县的山区竹林中。

黑龙江省的东北虎，是现在世界上老虎中体形最大的一种，可目前数量已经很少了。

东北虎

丹顶鹤是一种名贵的鹤，主要分布于黑龙江省，身高1.2米左右，体态秀丽，有"仙鹤"之称。

丹顶鹤

白鳍豚是淡水鲸的一种，

可爱的金丝猴

身体比鲸小,灰白色,只生活于中国的长江中。

还有生活在四川、云南、贵州等地的金丝猴,毛灰黄色,尾巴长,也是世界珍稀动物。

另外,在中国还生长着3万多种植物,占世界植物种类的1/10,其中有许多古老的植物品种,如闻名世界的珍贵树种水杉和银杏等。

在中国还有4,000多种药用植物,如人参(shēn)、三七等都是名贵的药材。

人参

千年银杏树

生词

tiáo jiàn 条件	condition		huī bái 灰白	ash grey
shǎn xī 陕西	Shaanxi (Province)		guì zhōu 贵州	Guizhou (Province)
gān sù 甘肃	Gansu (Province)		zhēn xī 珍稀	rare
dān dǐng hè 丹顶鹤	red-crowned crane		shuǐ shān 水杉	metasequoia
tǐ tài 体态	posture		yín xìng 银杏	ginkgo
xiù lì 秀丽	beautiful		zhēn guì 珍贵	valuable
jīng 鲸	whale		yào cái 药材	medicinal materials

听写

条件　　陕西　　甘肃　　体态　　秀丽　　鲸　　灰白

贵州　　珍贵　　药材　　*水杉　　银杏

反义词

珍贵——普通

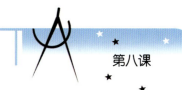

词语运用

条件

① 这里的学习条件很好,有个大图书馆。

② 张华的身体条件很好,跑得快,跳得高。

③ 中国的自然条件复杂。

回答问题

1. 中国有哪些珍稀动物？它们都生活在哪里？

2. 中国大约有多少种植物？

3. 我们应该怎样保护环境(hù huán jìng)？

阅读

银杏树——"活化石"

银杏树是中国的珍贵树种，它长得又高又大，叶子像一把小扇子，可活3,000年。

一亿多年前，地球上到处都有银杏树。冰川运动后，欧洲、美洲的银杏树被埋到地底，成了化石。只有一小部分在中国存活下来。科学家叫它"活化石"。

银杏树生长很慢，又叫"公孙树"，意思是爷爷种下的树，孙子才能吃到果实。银杏的果实叫白果，可以吃，也可以入药。

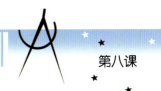

Wild Animals and Plants

The extensive territory of China contains many different habitats, which makes it one of countries with the richest resources of wildlife. There are many rare animals, such as the giant panda and the Changjiang dolphin.

The giant panda is a much beloved animal that lives in the bamboo forests of Sichuan, shaanxi and Gansu.

In Heilongjiang in the Northeast, the Siberian tiger roams, which is now the largest tiger on earth, but already very rare.

The red crowned crane is a rare crane that mostly lives in Heilongjiang. It is about 1.2 m tall, very elegant and therefore called the "immortal crane".

The Changjiang dolphin is a freshwater dolphin that is fairly small, greyish white and only lives in the Changjiang in China.

In Sichuan, Yunnan and Guizhou live the gold silk monkeys that have a golden coat and long tails and also belong to the rare animal on our globe.

In addition, there are 30,000 plant species in China, constituting 1/10 of all species worldwide. Many of these are ancient plants, such as the metasequoia and the ginko tree, two rare trees well known worldwide. There are some 4,000 medicinal plants in China, among which ginseng and noto-ginseng are among the most valued.

The Ginko: A Living Fossil

The ginko is a precious tree of China. It grows tall and large, has leaves shaped like small fans, and can live up to 3,000 years.

100 million years ago, ginko trees grew all over the world. After the ice age, they were buried under the glaciers, deep under the soil of Europe and America, where they became coal. Only some lived on in China. Scientists call the ginko a "living fossil."

The tree matures slowly and therefore is called the "grandfather-grandson tree." This means that if the grandfather planted a tree, his grandchildren will get to eat its fruit. The fruit of the ginko is called the "white fruit". It is edible and also used in medicines.

第九课
行政区划

中国现在的行政区分为：省（自治区、中央直辖市、特别行政区），市，县和乡（镇）几级。省级有23个省、5个自治区和4个直辖市，另外还有香港和澳门两个特别行政区。

北京是中国的首都，是中国的政治和文化中心。

中央直辖市有北京、上海、天津和重庆。

中国的23个省是：河北、山西、辽宁、吉林、黑龙江、山东、安徽、江苏、浙江、江西、福建、台湾、河南、湖北、湖南、广东、海南、四川、云南、贵州、陕西、甘肃和青海。

① 北京市
② 天津市
③ 宁夏回族自治区
④ 香港特别行政区
⑤ 澳门特别行政区

五个自治区是：广西壮族自治区、西藏自治区、内蒙古自治区、宁夏回族自治区和新疆维吾尔自治区。

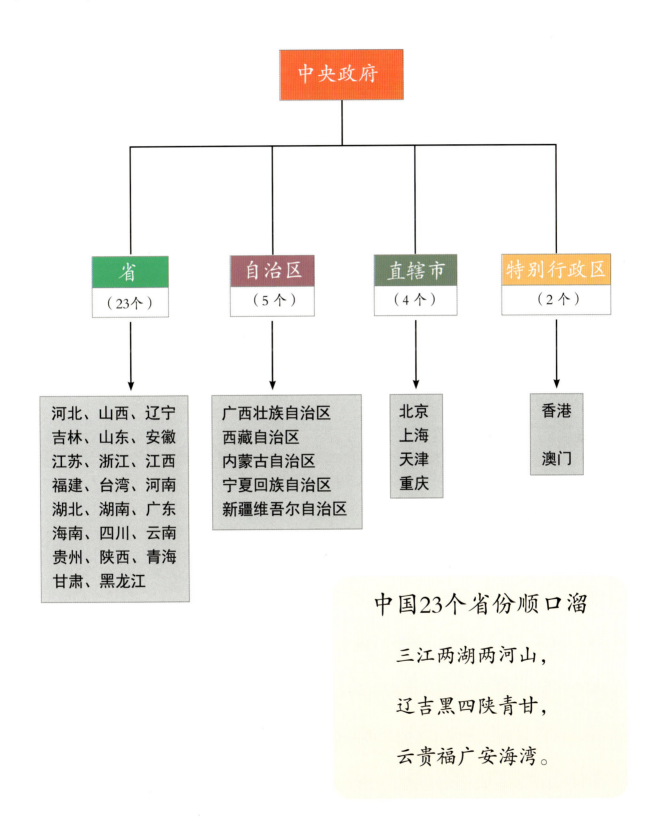

中国23个省份顺口溜

三江两湖两河山，

辽吉黑四陕青甘，

云贵福广安海湾。

生词

xíng zhèng 行政	administrative region	xiāng gǎng 香港	Hong Kong
qū huà 区划	partition	ào mén 澳门	Macau
shěng 省	province	shǒu dū 首都	capital
zì zhì qū 自治区	autonomous region	zhèng zhì 政治	politics, political
zhōng yāng 中央	central; center	chóng qìng 重庆	Chongqing
zhí xiá shì 直辖市	municipality directly under the Central Government	jí lín 吉林	Jilin (Province)
		níng xià 宁夏	Ningxia
zhèn 镇	town		

听写

行政区　　自治区　　省　　直辖市　　香港　　首都　　镇

三江两湖两河山，

辽吉黑四陕青甘，

云贵福广安海湾。

阅读

香港与澳门

香港是中国领土，原属广东省宝安县。1842年鸦片战争后，*香港岛割让给英国。1997年7月1日中国收回香港，把香港设为特别行政区。

香港是著名的国际金融、贸易中心和自由港口，也是著名的旅游城市、美食之都、购物天堂。

澳门在广东省南部，过去长期被葡萄牙占领，1999年12月20日中国收回澳门，把澳门设为特别行政区。

香港

---

*1842年鸦片战争后，清政府与英国签订不平等的《南京条约》，割让香港岛给英国。后又于1860年和1898年割让九龙半岛、租借新界给英国。

中国各省、直辖市、自治区简称表

省、市、自治区	简称	省、市、自治区	简称
北京	京	湖北	鄂(è)
天津	津	湖南	湘(xiāng)
河北	冀(jì)	广东	粤(yuè)
山西	晋(jìn)	广西	桂
内蒙古	蒙	海南	琼(qióng)
辽宁	辽	香港	港
吉林	吉	澳门	澳
黑龙江	黑	重庆	渝(yú)
上海	沪(hù)	四川	川或蜀(shǔ)
山东	鲁(lǔ)	云南	云或滇(diān)
安徽	皖(wǎn)	贵州	贵或黔(qián)
江苏	苏	西藏	藏
浙江	浙	陕西	陕或秦
江西	赣(gàn)	宁夏	宁
福建	闽(mǐn)	甘肃	甘或陇(lǒng)
台湾	台	青海	青
河南	豫(yù)	新疆	新

The Administrative Map of China

China has three levels of administrative subdivision: On top are the provinces (together with the autonomous regions, municipalities directly under the Central Government, and special administrative regions), under these are cities and districts, and on the lowest level are the counties (and towns). On the provincial level are 23 provinces, 5 autonomous regions and 4 municipalities directly under the Central Government. In addition, there are the two special administrative regions Hong Kong and Macao. Beijing is the capital of China and the political and cultural centre.

Beijing, Shanghai, Tianjin, and Chongqing are cities under direct administration.

The 23 provinces are: Hebei, Shanxi, Liaoning, Jilin, Heilongjiang, Shandong, Anhui, Jiangsu, Zhejiang, Jiangxi, Fujian, Taiwan, Henan, Hubei, Hunan, Guangdong, Hainan, Sichuan, Yunnan, Guizhou, Shaanxi, Gansu, and Qinghai.

The five autonomous regions are Guangxi Zhuang Autonomous Region, Tibet Autonomous Region, Inner Mongolia Autonomous Region, Ningxia Hui Autonomous Region and Xinjiang Uyghur Autonomous Region.

Hong Kong and Macao

Hong Kong is on the sovereign soil of China. In the past, it used to be part of Bao'an district in Guangdong. After the 1842 Opium War,* Hong Kong island was ceded to Great Britain. On July 1, 1997, it was returned to China and has since been a specially administrated region.

Hong Kong is a great center of finance and trade as well as a free port. It is also renowned as a tourist destination, a city of gourmet and a shopper's paradise.

Macao is in the south of Guangdong and has been occupied by Portugal for a long time. On December 20, 1999 Macao was restored to China and has since also been specially administrated region.

---

*After the Opium War, the Qing government and Great Britain concluded the Nanjing Treaty, in which Hong Kong island was ceded. In 1860 and 1989 Kowloon and the New Territories were leased to Great Britain.

第十课
著名城市
北 京

北京是中国的首都,她有三千年历史,是一个文明古都,又是一个美丽的现代化城市。

天安门

早在春秋战国时期,北京就是燕国的首都。12世纪后,元朝、明朝和清朝都定都北京。北京有许多名胜古迹,最著名的是长城、故宫、天坛和颐和园等。

故宫是明清两代的皇宫,位于北京的中心,建于1406年。故宫有9,999间半房子。一排排高大的宫殿,红墙黄瓦(wǎ),十分壮观。这里住过24位皇帝。

北京的街道十分整齐,

天坛

像个大棋盘。城中的古建筑四周多是红墙绿树，十分美丽。北京的许多街道还沿用古老的名称，如前门大街、米市大街、菜市口……

鸟巢

北京一直是中国的文化中心。这里有80多所大学，最有名的是北京大学和清华大学，还有国家图书馆和三百多家博物馆。

故宫

中国地理常识

生词

xiàn dài huà 现代化	modernization	zhuàng guān 壮观	magnificent
cháo 朝	dynasty	qí pán 棋盘	chessboard
míng shèng gǔ jì 名胜古迹	relic	jiàn zhù 建筑	architecture, construction
huáng gōng 皇宫	imperial palace	yán yòng 沿用	continue to use
gōng diàn 宫殿	palace	cài 菜	dish; vegetable

古迹名称

cháng chéng 长城	the Great Wall	tiān tán 天坛	the Temple of Heaven
gù gōng 故宫	the Imperial Palace	yí hé yuán 颐和园	the Summer Palace

听写

现代化　朝　名胜古迹　宫殿　棋盘　菜

*沿用

上 海

上海是中国最大的城市，位于长江入海处，交通方便，也是中国最大的海港。

上海古时是个县，近一百年来已发展成为中国人口最多、经济最发达的城市。

今日的上海是个现代化的大都市。银行、金融公司、贸易公司和工厂遍布上海。上海还有许多大学、剧院、商店、旅馆和餐厅。到了晚上，黄浦(pǔ)江边灯火通明。这一切，使繁华的大上海成为亚洲重要的金融、贸易和航运中心之一。

上海

中国地理常识

生词

jiāotōng 交通	traffic	gōng chǎng 工厂	factory
fā zhǎn 发展	develop	jù yuàn 剧院	theatre
yín háng 银行	bank	shāng diàn 商店	shop
jīn róng 金融	finance	lǚ guǎn 旅馆	hotel
gōng sī 公司	company	cān tīng 餐厅	restaurant
mào yì 贸易	trade	fán huá 繁华	prosperous

听写

交通　发展　银行　公司　工厂　剧院　贸易

商店　旅馆　*金融　餐厅

回答问题

1. 中国最大的城市是哪一个？

2. 中国的首都是哪儿？

3. 你去过北京吗？如果去过，说说你去过哪些地方。

4. 说说你知道的上海。

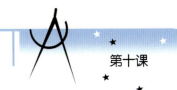

城市介绍

如何介绍城市(jiè shào)

1. 突出城市特点

2. 写作有条理(地理位置、城市特点、历史(zhì)、景观、居民生活一条条写)

3. 详略(xiáng lüè)得当(详细描述(miáo shù)一个特点或一件事)

文章结构

第一段	城市地理位置、特点
第二段	城市历史
第三段	市容、居民
第四段	描写市容或居民生活的一个特点(详细)
第五段	结尾扣题(kòu tí)

范文《旧金山》

提纲

第一段　旧金山位置：美国西海岸　　特点：著名的旅游城市

第二段　旧金山历史：淘金

第三段　景观建筑风格：西班牙式住房　街道高高低低

　　　　居民生活：移民多，文化多元

第四段　描述旧金山的多样性：中国城　法国角

第五段　结尾：旧金山让人难忘

旧金山

谢凯文（九年级）

旧金山在美国的西海岸，是个著名的旅游城市。在旧金山有许多"小城"如：中国城、日本城、法国角都非常有趣。

旧金山的"小城"和淘(táo)金的历史是分不开的。1848年的淘金热给旧金山带来了很多人口：中国人来了，日本人来了，法国人也来了。之后，就有了中国城、日本城、法国角。

旧金山建在海边的小山上，城市道路高高低低，路边的房屋多半是西班牙式的小楼，干净美丽。这里除了美国人以外，还住着来自欧洲、亚洲的移民，大家一起工作、生活。

如果有一天，你想出去玩儿，去哪儿才好呢？这个问题变得很容易，旧金山就是一个好地方。你可以先去看看金门大桥，再去法国角闻闻(wèi)法国面包的香味；然后去中国城听听外面的鞭炮(biān pào)声，尝尝(cháng)中国的大餐。如果还没有玩儿累的话，就去海边钓(diào)鱼。

旧金山去多少次都不会烦，总会发现新的有趣(qù)的地方。不信你就自己去瞧瞧(qiáo)吧。

Famous Cities

Beijing

Beijing is the capital of China. With its history of 3,000 years, it is an old cultural center as well as a great modern city.

Back in the Spring and Autumn and Warring States Period, Beijing used to be the capital of Yan. Since the 12th century, it had been the capital of the Yuan, the Ming and the Qing dynasties. There are many historic buildings and sites in and around Beijing, of which the best known are the Great Wall, the Forbidden City, the Temple of Heaven, and the Summer Palace.

The Forbidden City is the palace of the Ming and Qing emperors. It is located in the center of the city and was first built in 1604. There are 9,999 and a half rooms in the palace in many courtyards stacked one behind the other, surrounded by red walls and roofed under yellow tiles. 24 emperors resided here.

The street of Beijing follow a regular pattern, just like a chess board. Most old buildings in the city are surrounded by red walls and have green trees in their courtyards, very pleasant to live in. Many roads still have their old names, such as the Qianmen Road, the Rice Market Road, the Vegetable Market intersection …

Beijing has consistently been the cultural center of China. There are over 80 universities and colleges. The most prestigious are Peking University and Tsinghua University. In addition, the National Library and some 300 museums are found in this city.

颐和园长廊

Shanghai

Shanghai is the largest city in China. Located near the mouth of the Changjiang, it possesses convenient transportation and the largest ocean port of China.

In former times, Shanghai was a village. Over more than a century, it has developed into the most populous and economically leading city in China.

Today, Shanghai is a modern metropolis. It is a centre of banking, finance, trade, and industry. Moreover, there are numerous universities, theatres, shops, hotels and restaurants. In the evening, all along the Huangpu River, lights shine brightly. This flourishing city is a hub of finance, trade and transport in Asia.

第十一课
中国名山（选修课）

泰　山

五岳独尊(zūn)的泰山，在中国山东省中部，海拔1,545米，是中国第一名山。泰山名气大，也因为几千年来很多皇帝来泰山朝拜。这里有许多古代建筑和2,000多处古人的石刻，走在山中，就好像走在书法艺术的博物馆里。泰山风景秀丽，著名的玉皇顶可以看日出和云海。

泰山日出

黄　山

奇美黄山

中国是个多山的国家，其中黄山最为奇美。黄山在安徽省南部，是著名的旅游胜地。黄山之美，在于有奇松、怪石、云海和温泉。著名的"迎客松"至少已有800年了。黄山还有许多怪石，有的像莲(lián)花，有的像猴子观海。山峰之间，白云像海水一样。

桂林山水

人们都说："桂林山水甲天下"，"甲"在这里是第一的意思。桂林在广西壮族自治区，是个美丽的小城。而桂林最美的景色又是漓(lí)江。漓江长160千米，是世界上最秀美的河流之一，河水清澈(chè)透明，真是"群峰倒影山浮水，无水无山不入神"。人们坐着小船在漓江上，就像进入仙境之中。

桂林山水甲天下

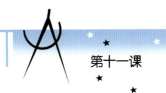

生词

tài shān 泰山	Mount tai	yíng kè sōng 迎客松	the pine greeting guests
cháo bài 朝拜	worship	shān fēng 山峰	mountain peaks
shí kè 石刻	stone carving	guì lín 桂林	Guilin
shū fǎ 书法	calligraphy	jiǎ 甲	number one
yì shù 艺术	art	dào yǐng 倒影	reflection
fēng jǐng 风景	scenery	fú 浮	float
lǚ yóu 旅游	tourism	xiān jìng 仙境	wonderland

听写

泰山　书法　艺术　风景　旅游　山峰　甲　倒影

泰山石刻

公元前219年,秦始皇巡游泰山,丞相李斯将秦始皇统一中国的功德刻于泰山。之后2,200多年,许多帝王、书法家、名人都在泰山留下自己的书法作品:诗、文、题字等,使泰山石刻越来越丰富了。不论是小篆、隶书、楷书、草书都有佳作。书法美,含义深,让一块块石头活了起来。一座风光秀丽的泰山,慢慢变成了石刻书法艺术的博物馆。

(清)光绪：五岳独尊

泰山,是自然遗产,也是文化遗产,世界独一无二。

秦:李斯

泰山石刻群

Mount Tai

Mount Tai is in the middle of Shandong province, and its peak is 1,545 m tall. It ranks first among the famous mountains of China. This is because emperors had come to worship at this mountain for several thousand years. There are hundreds of historic buildings and over 2,000 inscriptions carved in stone. A hike on this mountain is much like a visit to a calligraphy museum. The landscape is beautiful; from the Jade Emperor Peak you can watch the sunrise over the sea of clouds…

Mount Huang

There are many mountains in China, Mount Huang stands out for its bizarre beauty. This famous tourist site is located in the South of Anhui and a great tourist attraction. Its beauty lies in the strangely shaped pines and rocks, the sea of clouds and hot springs. There is a "pine that welcomes the guests," which is at least 800 years old. There are groups of rocks that resemble lotus flowers and others that look like monkeys looking out at the sea. White clouds between peaks look like ocean waters.

The Hills and Waters of Guilin

It is said that "the Guilin landscape is unsurpassed under the skies." Guilin is a small city in Guangxi Zhuang Autonomous Region. On the banks of the Lijiang, it is surrounded by one of the world's most famous scenic areas. For 160 km, the clear river meanders between limestone cones, forming a landscape where "Peaks are reflections floating in the water," each mountain and each water body is a marvel. When you sit in a small boat on the Lijiang, you might think that you have entered the land of immortals.

The Inscriptions of Mount Tai

In 219 BC, the First Emperor travelled to Mount Tai, and his minister Li Si penned an inscription in seal script that praised the merits of the emperor in unifying China and Li carved it on the mountain. In the following 2,200 years, numerous emperors, calligraphers and poets left their works on the mountains, making the rocks come to life with poems, essays, and captions. There are inscriptions in small seas script, clerical script, regular script and cursive, embodying the aesthetics of calligraphy and deep meaning to the natural beauty of the mountain. The art of calligraphy was thus gradually added, transforming the mountain into a museum of calligraphy.

Mount Tai is a site of natural beauty and at once a cultural relic, which makes it unique in the world.

第十二课
名胜古迹（选修课）

万里长城

长城建于2,000多年前的春秋战国时期，是古代的军事工程。长城东起山海关（河北），西到嘉峪(jiā yù)关（甘肃），经过辽宁、河北、北京、山西、内蒙古、陕西、宁夏、甘肃，全长6,700多千米（13,400里），也叫万里长城。长城每隔一段就有一个烽火台，

长城

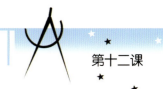

如果有敌人来,烽火台白天放烟,夜间点火;台台相连,传递消息,是最古老的"土电报",也是古代传递军情的好办法。

烽火台点燃狼烟

秦兵马俑

1974年,在中国西安发现了2,000多年前秦始皇陵中的兵马俑,出土兵俑、车马等共8,000多件,是中国著名的古迹之一。

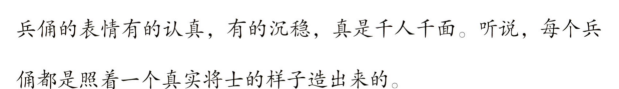

秦兵马俑

出土的兵俑真人大小,有将军俑、骑兵俑、步兵俑等。兵俑的表情有的认真,有的沉稳,真是千人千面。听说,每个兵俑都是照着一个真实将士的样子造出来的。

出土的铜马车也很精美,由3,462个大小不同的青铜、黄金、白银的零件组成。

中国地理常识

秦兵马俑

生词

jūn shì 军事	military	diàn bào 电报	telegraph
fēng huǒ tái 烽火台	beacon tower	líng 陵	mausoleum
dí rén 敌人	enemy	biǎo qíng 表情	expression
yān 烟	smoke	chén wěn 沉稳	composed
chuán dì 传递	pass	tóng 铜	copper
xiāo xi 消息	message	líng jiàn 零件	parts

听写

传递　消息　古迹　沉稳　铜　零件

数笔画

| 弟 | 第 | 递 |

＿＿＿画　　＿＿＿画　　＿＿＿画

比一比

程 { 工程 / 路程

情 { 表情 / 心情

沉 { 沉稳 / 下沉

{ 弟（弟弟）/ 第（第一）/ 递（传递）

阅读

有趣的兵俑

参观秦兵马俑，你会看到多种不同的兵俑。

将军俑，共出土9件，他们胸前和肩上都有花结，是指挥官。骑兵俑，出土116件，他们一手牵马，一手拿弓。出土最多的是步兵俑和跪射俑。跪射俑身穿铠甲，一条腿跪着，翻出的鞋底上还有针脚。乐舞俑出土30多件，他们大多光着上身。最后还有文官俑，他们戴着和将军俑一样的帽子。兵俑表情真实生动。

秦兵俑图

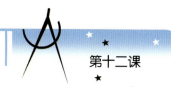

The Great Wall

The Great Wall was first built 2,000 years ago in the Spring and Autumn and Warring States Period as part of ancient military engineering.

The Great Wall extends from the Shanhai Pass (Hebei) to the Jiayu Pass (Gansu) across 6,700 km (or 13,400 li) through Liaoning, Hebei, Beijing, Shanxi, Inner Mongolia, Shaanxi, Ningxia, and Gansu. It is also called the "10,000 li Wall." After each section of the wall, there is a beacon. When enemies approached, the beacon fire was lit, using smoke during daytime and fire at night, spreading the message from beacon tower to beacon tower. This is an ancient precursor of the telegraph and an efficient means of military communication.

The Terracotta Army of the First Emperor

In 1974, the army of terracotta soldiers, horses and carriages was discovered in the grave of the First Emperor near Xi'an. Some 8,000 figures have been excavated at the site.

The soldiers are about as tall as real humans. There are generals, cavalry and infantry soldiers. Some diligent, some grave, they all are expressive as thousands of living men would be. It is said that each was modelled on a real warrior. Among the excavated objects, bronze carriages are also exquiste, which are made from 3,462 bronze, gold, and silver parts.

Interesting Facts about the Terracotta Warriors

When you visit the Terracotta Army, you will find many different figures.

Nine generals have been excavated, with elaborate breast and shoulder knots. These were the men in command. There are 116 cavalry soldiers, with one hand leading the horse and another holding the bow. The majority are infantry soldiers and kneeling archers. The archers wear armour and kneel on one knee. On the dropped back foot you can see the spikes on the sole of their shoes, which prevented slipping. There are also some 30 musicians, mostly with bare upper bodies, and a civilian official who wears a cap that is similar to that of the generals. All these figures look lively and expressive.

生字表（简）

1. 洲(zhōu) 岸(àn) 广(guǎng) 阔(kuò) 陆(lù) 积(jī) 欧(ōu) 蒙(měng) 度(dù) 隔(gé) 线(xiàn) 屿(yǔ)
2. 族(zú) 界(jiè) 亿(yì) 占(zhàn) 均(jūn) 汉(hàn) 维(wéi) 吾(wú) 尔(ěr) 藏(zàng) 区(qū) 寿(shòu) 免(miǎn) 费(fèi)
3. 势(shì) 阶(jiē) 脉(mài) 昆(kūn) 仑(lún) 横(héng) 寒(hán) 泊(pō) 内(nèi) 肥(féi) 层(céng)
4. 沃(wò) 津(jīn) 浙(zhè) 江(jiāng) 稠(chóu) 密(mì) 济(jì) 达(dá) 塔(tǎ) 降(jiàng) 润(rùn)
5. 源(yuán) 称(chēng) 副(fù) 域(yù) 繁(fán) 荣(róng) 运(yùn) 丰(fēng) 富(fù) 资(zī) 库(kù)
6. 杂(zá) 炎(yán) 集(jí) 差(chā) 燥(zào) 纬(wěi) 属(shǔ)
7. 产(chǎn) 稻(dào) 棉(mián) 遍(biàn) 疆(jiāng) 取(qǔ) 元(yuán) 徽(huī) 品(pǐn) 类(lèi)
8. 陕(shǎn) 甘(gān) 肃(sù) 丹(dān) 顶(dǐng) 鹤(hè) 态(tài) 秀(xiù) 鲸(jīng) 珍(zhēn) 杉(shān) 杏(xìng) 药(yào) 材(cái)
9. 政(zhèng) 划(huà) 央(yāng) 辖(xiá) 镇(zhèn) 港(gǎng) 澳(ào) 首(shǒu) 庆(qìng) 吉(jí) 宁(níng)
10. 朝(cháo) 迹(jì) 皇(huáng) 宫(gōng) 殿(diàn) 棋(qí) 筑(zhù) 沿(yán) 菜(cài) 交(jiāo) 展(zhǎn) 融(róng)

	sī	mào	chǎng	lǚ	cān				
	司	贸	厂	旅	餐				
	tài	bài	yì	jǐng	kè	fēng	guì	jiǎ	fú	jìng
11.	泰	拜	艺	景	客	峰	桂	甲	浮	境
	fēng	dí	yān	dì	xiāo	líng	wěn	tóng	líng
12.	烽	敌	烟	递	消	陵	稳	铜	零

共计137个生字，累计1279个生字

生字表（繁）

1. 洲(zhōu) 岸(àn) 廣(guǎng) 闊(kuò) 陸(lù) 積(jī) 歐(ōu) 蒙(měng) 度(dù) 隔(gé) 綫(xiàn) 嶼(yǔ)
2. 族(zú) 界(jiè) 億(yì) 占(zhàn) 均(jūn) 漢(hàn) 維(wéi) 吾(wú) 爾(ěr) 藏(zàng) 區(qū) 壽(shòu) 免(miǎn) 費(fèi)
3. 勢(shì) 階(jiē) 脉(mài) 崑(kūn) 崙(lún) 橫(héng) 寒(hán) 泊(pō) 內(nèi) 肥(féi) 層(céng)
4. 沃(wò) 津(jīn) 浙(zhè) 江(jiāng) 稠(chóu) 密(mì) 濟(jì) 達(dá) 塔(tǎ) 降(jiàng) 潤(rùn)
5. 源(yuán) 稱(chēng) 副(fù) 域(yù) 繁(fán) 榮(róng) 運(yùn) 豐(fēng) 富(fù) 資(zī) 庫(kù)
6. 雜(zá) 炎(yán) 集(jí) 差(chā) 燥(zào) 緯(wěi) 屬(shǔ)
7. 產(chǎn) 稻(dào) 棉(mián) 遍(biàn) 疆(jiāng) 取(qǔ) 元(yuán) 徽(huī) 品(pǐn) 類(lèi)
8. 陝(shǎn) 甘(gān) 肅(sù) 丹(dān) 頂(dǐng) 鶴(hè) 態(tài) 秀(xiù) 鯨(jīng) 珍(zhēn) 杉(shān) 杏(xìng) 藥(yào) 材(cái)
9. 政(zhèng) 劃(huà) 央(yāng) 轄(xiá) 鎮(zhèn) 港(gǎng) 澳(ào) 首(shǒu) 慶(qìng) 吉(jí) 寧(níng)
10. 朝(cháo) 迹(jì) 皇(huáng) 宮(gōng) 殿(diàn) 棋(qí) 築(zhù) 沿(yán) 菜(cài) 交(jiāo) 展(zhǎn) 融(róng)

	sī	mào	chǎng	lǚ	cān				
	司	貿	廠	旅	餐				
	tài	bài	yì	jǐng	kè	fēng	guì	jiǎ	fú	jìng
11.	泰	拜	藝	景	客	峰	桂	甲	浮	境
	fēng	dí	yān	dì	xiāo	líng	wěn	tóng	líng
12.	烽	敵	烟	遞	消	陵	穩	銅	零

共計137個生字，纍計1279個生字

生词表（简）

1. 亚洲（yà zhōu） 位于（wèi yú） 地球（dì qiú） 东部（dōng bù） 太平洋（tài píng yáng） 西岸（xī àn） 领土（lǐng tǔ） 广阔（guǎng kuò） 陆地（lù dì） 面积（miàn jī） 平方（píng fāng） 欧洲（ōu zhōu） 蒙古（měng gǔ） 印度（yìn dù） 隔海相望（gé hǎi xiāng wàng） 海岸线（hǎi àn xiàn） 岛屿（dǎo yǔ）

2. 人口（rén kǒu） 民族（mín zú） 世界（shì jiè） 亿（yì） 占（zhàn） 分布（fēn bù） 平均（píng jūn） 居住（jū zhù） 汉族（hàn zú） 其他（qí tā） 维吾尔族（wéi wú ěr zú） 藏族（zàng zú） 地区（dì qū） 寿命（shòu mìng） 免费（miǎn fèi）

3. 高原（gāo yuán） 地势（dì shì） 阶梯（jiē tī） 山脉（shān mài） 昆仑山（kūn lún shān） 横断山（héng duàn shān） 海拔（hǎi bá） 高寒（gāo hán） 湖泊（hú pō） 内蒙古（nèi měng gǔ） 肥美（féi měi） 土层（tǔ céng） 平原（píng yuán）

4. 盆地（pén dì） 肥沃（féi wò） 天津（tiān jīn） 浙江（zhè jiāng） 稠密（chóu mì） 经济（jīng jì） 发达（fā dá） 降水（jiàng shuǐ） 内（nèi） 通道（tōng dào） 气候（qì hòu） 湿润（shī rùn） 农业（nóng yè）

5. 长江（cháng jiāng） 黄河（huáng hé） 发源（fā yuán） 流经（liú jīng） 文明（wén míng） 称为（chēng wéi） 名副其实（míng fù qí shí） 流域（liú yù） 繁荣（fán róng） 航运（háng yùn） 丰富（fēng fù） 资源（zī yuán） 水库（shuǐ kù）

6. 复杂（fù zá） 特点（tè diǎn） 季风（jì fēng） 普遍（pǔ biàn） 影响（yǐng xiǎng） 炎热（yán rè） 因此（yīn cǐ） 降雨（jiàng yǔ） 集中（jí zhōng） 温差（wēn chā） 干燥（gān zào） 纬度（wěi dù） 法国（fǎ guó） 属于（shǔ yú）

生词表（简）

7. 物产(wù chǎn) 农作物(nóng zuò wù) 水稻(shuǐ dào) 棉花(mián huā) 谷子(gǔ zi) 遍布(biàn bù) 新疆(xīn jiāng) 产量(chǎn liàng) 取(qǔ) 闻名天下(wén míng tiān xià) 故乡(gù xiāng) 公元(gōng yuán) 安徽(ān huī) 福建(fú jiàn) 品质(pǐn zhì) 种类(zhǒng lèi)

8. 条件(tiáo jiàn) 陕西(shǎn xī) 甘肃(gān sù) 丹顶鹤(dān dǐng hè) 体态(tǐ tài) 秀丽(xiù lì) 鲸(jīng) 灰白(huī bái) 贵州(guì zhōu) 珍稀(zhēn xī) 水杉(shuǐ shān) 银杏(yín xìng) 珍贵(zhēn guì) 药材(yào cái)

9. 行政(xíng zhèng) 区划(qū huà) 省(shěng) 自治区(zì zhì qū) 中央(zhōng yāng) 直辖市(zhí xiá shì) 镇(zhèn) 香港(xiāng gǎng) 澳门(ào mén) 首都(shǒu dū) 政治(zhèng zhì) 重庆(chóng qìng) 吉林(jí lín) 宁夏(níng xià)

10. 现代化(xiàn dài huà) 朝(cháo) 名胜古迹(míng shèng gǔ jì) 皇宫(huáng gōng) 宫殿(gōng diàn) 壮观(zhuàng guān) 棋盘(qí pán) 建筑(jiàn zhù) 沿用(yán yòng) 菜(cài) 交通(jiāo tōng) 发展(fā zhǎn) 银行(yín háng) 金融(jīn róng) 公司(gōng sī) 贸易(mào yì) 工厂(gōng chǎng) 剧院(jù yuàn) 商店(shāng diàn) 旅馆(lǚ guǎn) 餐厅(cān tīng) 繁华(fán huá)

11. 泰山(tài shān) 朝拜(cháo bài) 石刻(shí kè) 书法(shū fǎ) 艺术(yì shù) 风景(fēng jǐng) 旅游(lǚ yóu) 迎客松(yíng kè sōng) 山峰(shān fēng) 桂林(guì lín) 甲(jiǎ) 倒影(dào yǐng) 浮(fú) 仙境(xiān jìng)

12. 军事(jūn shì) 烽火台(fēng huǒ tái) 敌人(dí rén) 烟(yān) 传递(chuán dì) 消息(xiāo xi) 电报(diàn bào) 陵(líng) 表情(biǎo qíng) 沉稳(chén wěn) 铜(tóng) 零件(líng jiàn)

共计179个生词

生词表（繁）

1. 亞洲 位於 地球 東部 太平洋 西岸 領土 廣闊 陸地 面積 平方 歐洲 蒙古 印度 隔海相望 海岸綫 島嶼

2. 人口 民族 世界 億 占 分布 平均 居住 漢族 其他 維吾爾族 藏族 地區 壽命 免費

3. 高原 地勢 階梯 山脈 崑崙山 橫斷山 海拔 高寒 湖泊 內蒙古 肥美 土層 平原

4. 盆地 肥沃 天津 浙江 稠密 經濟 發達 降水 內 通道 氣候 濕潤 農業

5. 長江 黃河 發源 流經 文明 稱爲 名副其實 流域 繁榮 航運 豐富 資源 水庫

6. 複雜 特點 季風 普遍 影響 炎熱 因此 降雨 集中 溫差 乾燥 緯度 法國 屬於

7. 物產 農作物 水稻 棉花 穀子 遍布 新疆 產量 取 聞名天下 故鄉 公元 安徽 福建 品質 種類

8. 條件 陝西 甘肅 丹頂鶴 體態 秀麗 鯨 灰白 貴州 珍稀 水杉 銀杏 珍貴 藥材

9. 行政 區劃 省 自治區 中央 直轄市 鎮 香港 澳門 首都 政治 重慶 吉林 寧夏

10. 現代化 朝 名勝古迹 皇宮 宮殿 壯觀 棋盤 建築 沿用 菜 交通 發展 銀行 金融 公司 貿易 工廠 劇院 商店 旅館 餐廳 繁華

11. 泰山 朝拜 石刻 書法 藝術 風景 旅游 迎客松 山峰 桂林 甲 倒影 浮 仙境

12. 軍事 烽火臺 敵人 烟 傳遞 消息 電報 陵 表情 沉穩 銅 零件

共計179個生詞

附录

"新双双中文教材"写作练习（1—7册）

课文正式教授写作内容

内容	出处	建议学习年级
1．课文缩写	第4册 《猴子捞月亮》	3—4年级
2．日记	第5册 《妈妈教我写日记》	4—5年级
3．叙事文	第5册 《参观兵马俑》	4—5年级
4．看图写故事	第6册 成语故事《塞翁失马》	5—6年级
5．城市介绍	第7册 中国地理常识《著名城市》	5—6年级

辅助写作练习

内容	出处	建议学习年级
1．读书笔记	亲子阅读，每周家庭读书、写作	2—6年级
2．观察记录	第4册 写《养蚕报告》	3—4年级
3．创作	写简单的故事和想法	4年级以上

中国政区图

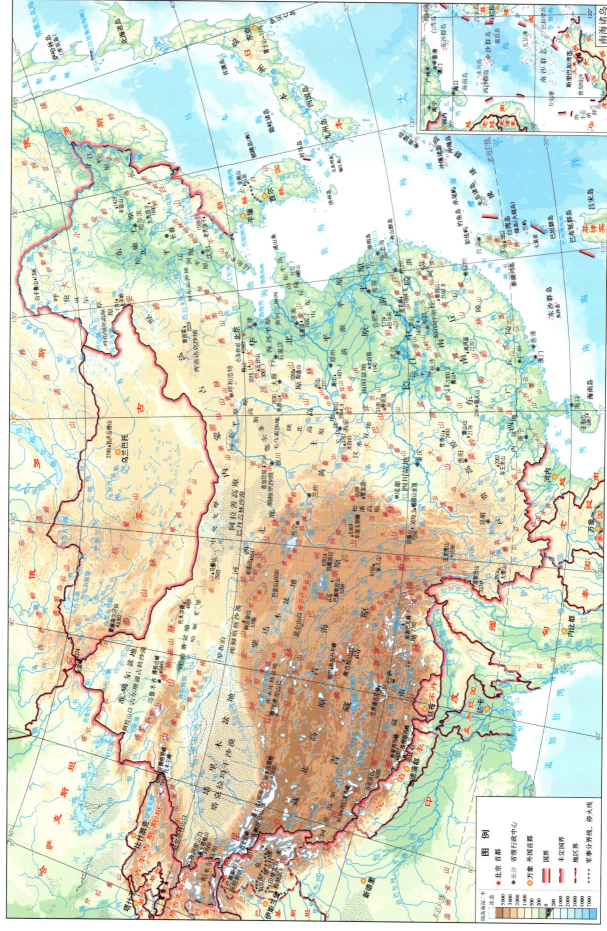

中国地形图

新双双中文教材 7

New Chinese Language and Culture Course

中国地理常识 Common Chinese Geography Textbook

练习本 单课

石雪丽 编著

北京大学出版社
PEKING UNIVERSITY PRESS

NanHai
BRIDGING EAST & WEST

目　录

第一课　亚洲最大的国家 …………………………………… 1

第三课　山地和高原 ………………………………………… 5

第五课　江河与湖泊 ………………………………………… 9

第七课　农作物和名产 ……………………………………… 13

第九课　行政区划 …………………………………………… 17

第十一课　中国名山（选修课） …………………………… 22

第一课 亚洲最大的国家

练习一　　　练习二　　　练习三

一　写生词

亚	洲		

位	于		

地	球		

东	部		

西	岸		

领	土		

二　组词

洲_____　　亚_____　　球_____　　部_____

位_____　　地_____　　岸_____　　领_____

三　下面的图哪个是中国？把中国涂成红色。其他的图，如果你认识，请写出国名

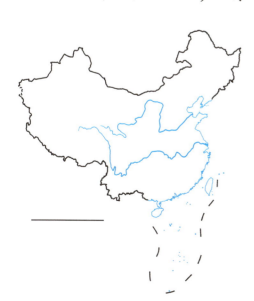

第一课 亚洲最大的国家

练习一　　练习二　　练习三

一　写生词

广	阔		

陆	地		

面	积		

太	平	洋		

海	岸	线		

隔	海	相	望		
平	方				

岛	屿		

二　组词

积_____　　屿_____　　陆_____　　线_____

三　选择填空

1. 中国位于地球的_____，亚洲的东部，太平洋的_____。（北半球　南半球）（东岸　西岸）

2. 中国陆地总面积_____万平方千米，是亚洲_____的国家。（960　690）（最大　最热）

第一课 亚洲最大的国家

练习一　　练习二　　**练习三**

一　写生词

蒙	古		

印	度		

欧	洲		

二　用圆圈里的字，加上部首，会变成哪个字？再用那个字组词

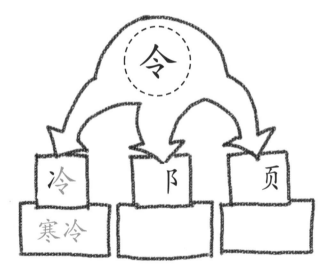

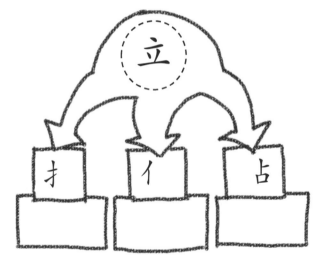

三　多看地图，熟悉地图后排列

1. 从大到小排列

亚洲　中国
北半球　地球

2. 从北向南排列

蒙古　俄罗斯
中国　越南

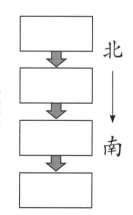

北 → 南

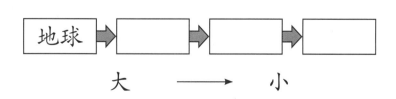

大　——　小

第一课 亚洲最大的国家

练习一　　练习二　　**练习三**

四 填图

1. 在图上填出中国的陆上邻国（6个以上）（朝鲜　越南　蒙古　印度　俄罗斯　尼泊尔　缅甸　巴基斯坦）。

2. 在图上填出与中国隔海相望的国家（3个以上）（韩国　日本　菲律宾）。

3. 环绕中国陆地的海是图上的 ❶_____，❷_____，❸_____，❹_____

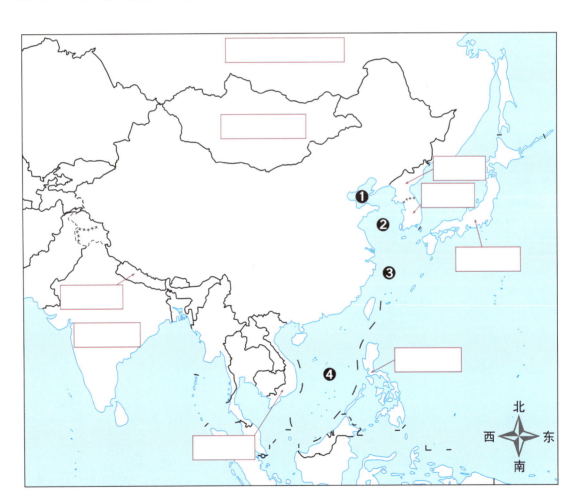

五 朗读课文三遍，记下你每次用了多长时间

1. _____　　2. _____　　3. _____

第三课 山地和高原

练习一　　练习二　　练习三

一　写生词

高	原		

地	势		

阶	梯		

山	脉		

海	拔		

高	寒		

二　连线找到另一半，看你得到了什么字，再用它组词

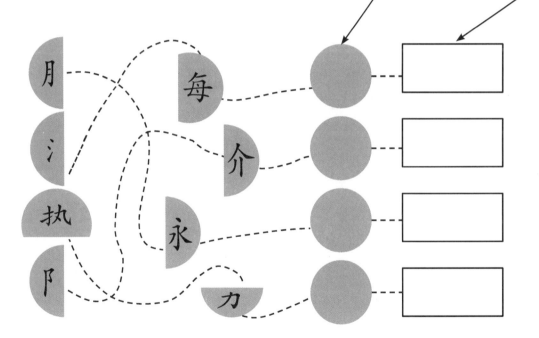

左半：月、氵、执、阝
右半：每、介、永、力

三　选择填空

1. 中国的地势是_____。（西高东低　东高西低）

2. 中国的山地和高原____全国面积的____。

（站　占）（2/3　1/2）

第三课 山地和高原

练习一　★练习二　☆练习三

一　写生词

湖	泊

肥	美

土	层

平	原

昆	仑	山

横	断	山

内	蒙	古

二　选词填空

> 雪山　青藏高原　黄土高原　肥美

1. 青藏高原上有许多高大的_____。

2. _____地表是厚厚的黄土层。

3. _____海拔多在4,000米以上。

4. 内蒙古高原的许多地方，水草_____，牛羊成群。

第三课 山地和高原

练习一　练习二　★ 练习三

一　看第14页地图，填出高原名称和主要山脉名称

❶ _____ 山　❷ _____　❸ _____　❹ _____

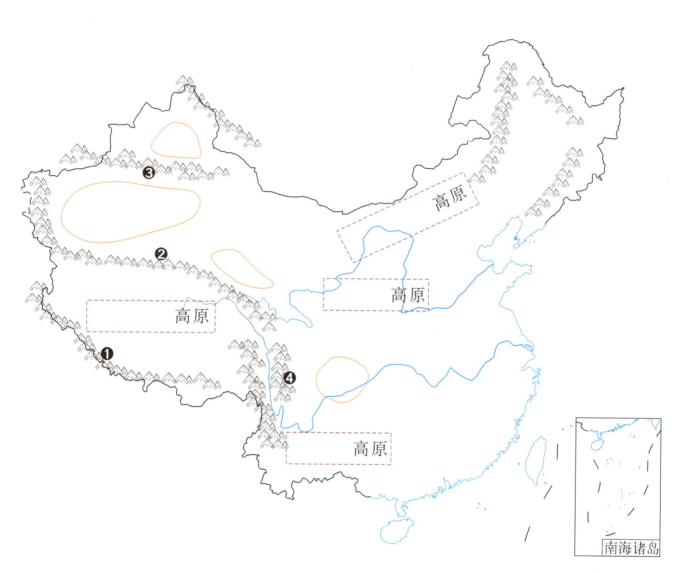

二　朗读课文三遍，记下你每次用了多长时间

1. _____　2. _____　3. _____

第三课 山地和高原

练习一　　练习二　　**练习三**

三　上网搜索后填写

1. 我居住的地方海拔高度是_____米。

2. 在我居住的国家，海拔最高的山是_____，海拔_____米。

四　根据《布达拉宫》和《牦牛——高原之舟》选择填空

1. 50元人民币上的照片是西藏的_____。

（布达拉宫　故宫）

2. 布达拉宫有_____历史，是_____的文化中心。

（300年　1,300年）（汉族　藏族）

3. 布达拉宫海拔_____。（370米　3,700米）

4. 青藏高原的_____被称为高原之舟。（马　牦牛）

5. 高原的藏民做饭和取暖烧的是_____。

（干木柴　干牦牛粪）

第五课 江河与湖泊

练习一 ★　　　练习二 ☆　　　练习三 ☆

一　写生词

长	江

黄	河

发	源

流	经

文	明

称	为

流	域

繁	荣

名	副	其	实

二　组词

黄_____　　繁_____　　江_____　　源_____

发_____　　称_____　　流_____　　原_____

三　选择填空

1. 黄河和长江都发源于青藏高_____。（原　源）

2. 黄河是中国古代文明的发_____地。（原　源）

3. 中国的三大平_____都在东部。（原　源）

第五课 江河与湖泊

练习一　★练习二　练习三

一　写生词

航	运

丰	富

资	源

水	库

二　新学的"氵"的字有很多，你记得哪些？再用那个字组词。

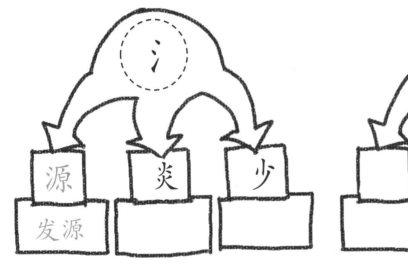
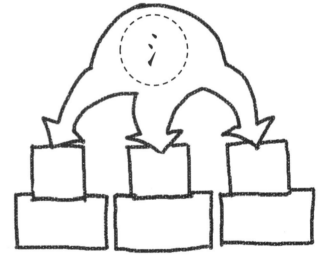

三　填空

1. 中国第一大河是 _____，第二是 _____。

2. 黄河位于中国的____部。长江是世界第____大河。

第五课 江河与湖泊

练习一　　练习二　　★ 练习三

一　填出长江、黄河

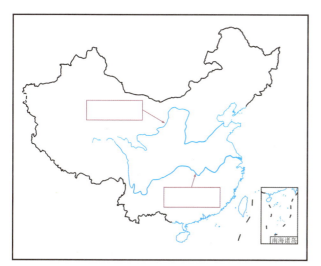

你觉得中国地图的形状像什么？画一张中国地图，可以把地图加工成你想象的东西⬇⬇⬇

二　选择填空

1. _____是咸水湖。（青海湖　洞庭湖）

2. _____被称为中国古代文明的发源地。

（黄河　黑龙江）

3. 江西的_____的水量变化大，像是长江的水库，湖南的_____是中国第二大淡水湖。（洞庭湖　鄱阳湖）

三　上网搜索后填写

1. 我居住的国家的第一大河是_____，长_____千米

2. 世界第一大河是_____，第二是_____，第三是长江，第四是_____，第五是_____。

第五课 江河与湖泊

练习一　　练习二　　**练习三**

四　读一读，用画线的词语造句

　　长江，是一条<u>名副其实</u>的长河。

　　名副其实_____。

五　根据《黄河的"地上河"》回答问题

　　1. 黄河下游是怎样变成"地上河"的？

　　_____

　　_____

　　2. 写出4个黄河流经的省_____

六　比较中国最著名的两条河：黄河、长江

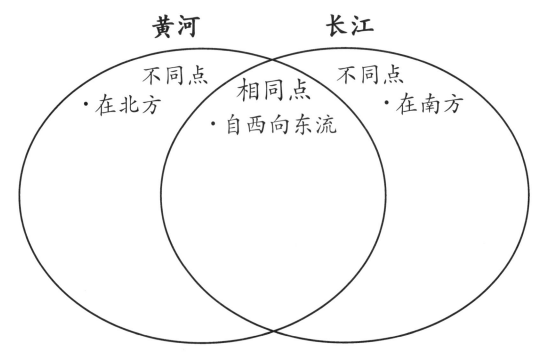

黄河　　　　　长江

不同点　　相同点　　不同点
·在北方　　·自西向东流　　·在南方

第七课 农作物和名产

★ 练习一 ☆ 练习二 ☆ 练习三

一　写生词

物	产		

水	稻		

棉	花		

农	作	物		

闻	名	天	下		

二　你知道这些农作物的中文名字吗？请写出。它们可以做成什么食品？请连线。

Millet  谷子

Rice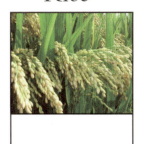

Soybean

Wheat

 小米粥

第七课 农作物和名产

练习一　　练习二　　练习三

一　写生词

谷	子		

遍	布		

新	疆		

产	量		

故	乡		

安	徽		

福	建		

品	质		

种	类		

二　选择填空

1. 中国是有着_____农业文明的国家。

（6,000年　1,000年）

2. 中国的水稻产量占世界总产量的_____。（1/3　19%）

3. 中国的棉花产量占世界总产量的_____。（1/3　27%）

4. 中国5,000年前就开始养蚕取丝，被称为_____。

（丝绸之乡　丝绸之路）

5. 中国茶品质上好，有_____、_____、_____等种类。（红茶　绿茶　奶茶　花茶）

第七课 农作物和名产

练习一　　练习二　　★ 练习三

一　写生词

二　组词

农_____　物_____　遍_____　豆_____

稻_____　量_____　新_____　产_____

三　根据《茶》《稻田养鱼》选择填空

1. 传说是_____发现了茶可以喝，可以解毒。

（神农　农业）

2. 中国的茶园主要在_____。（北方　南方）

3. 茶是_____的饮料。（健康　传说）

4. 稻田养鱼，就是在种_____时，在田里养鱼。

（谷子　水稻）

5. 田里的鱼会吃_____和小虫，鱼粪又成为水稻的_____。（复杂　肥料　杂草）

四　朗读课文三遍

| 第七课 农作物和名产 | 练习一 | 练习二 | 练习三 |

五　你住的地方，附近有农田吗？农田里种的是什么农作物？你居住的国家有哪些特产和名产？

_____

_____

六　用一句话写出照片里有什么，照片里的人在做什么

1.

_____

2.

_____

3.

_____

4.

_____

第九课 行政区划

★ 练习一　　☆ 练习二　　☆ 练习三

一 写生词

行	政	区

直	辖	市

中	央

首	都

二 组词

行_____　　央_____　　省_____　　吉_____

直_____　　首_____　　市_____　　政_____

三 填空

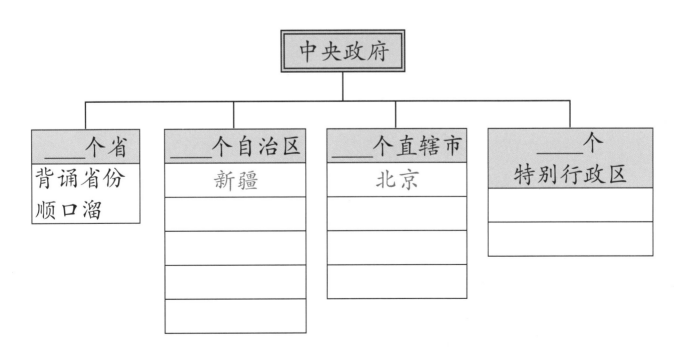

第九课 行政区划

练习二

一 写生词

自	治	区

政	治

划

省

镇

二 背诵23个省份顺口溜，把下面被挡住的字补好

```
二 江 西 湖 西 河 小
辽 吉 黑 四 陕 青 甘
云 贵 福 广 安 海 湾
```

三 朗读课文三遍，再回答问题

- 如果你去过中国，写一下你去过哪些地方。

- 如果你没去过，你觉得哪个省/市/自治区/特别行政区的名字最好听/好记？

第九课 行政区划

练习一　练习二　**练习三**

一　写生词

香	港

澳	门

重	庆

吉	林

宁	夏

二　多看地图，熟悉地图后选择填空

1. 下面每组地名中，不相邻的是_____。

　　A. 山东　山西　　　B. 河南　河北　　　C. 湖南　湖北

2. 下面地名中，没有海岸线的是_____。

　　A. 上海　　　　　　B. 青海　　　　　　C. 海南

3. 黄河没有流过_____。

　　A. 宁夏　　　　　　B. 山西　　　　　　C. 河北

第九课 行政区划

练习一　练习二　**练习三**

三　多看地图，熟悉地图后排列

1. 按面积，从大到小排列

新疆 ➡ ☐ ➡ ☐ ➡ ☐

大 ——— 小

2. 从北向南排列

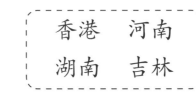

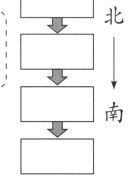

北 ——— 南

3. 从西到东排列

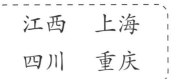

☐ ➡ ☐ ➡ ☐ ➡ ☐

西 ——— 东

4. 按海拔，从高到低排列

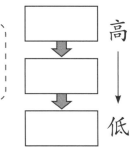

高 ——— 低

第九课 行政区划

练习一　练习二　**练习三**

四　这些地图的形状像什么？发挥你的想象，把它画成你想的东西。

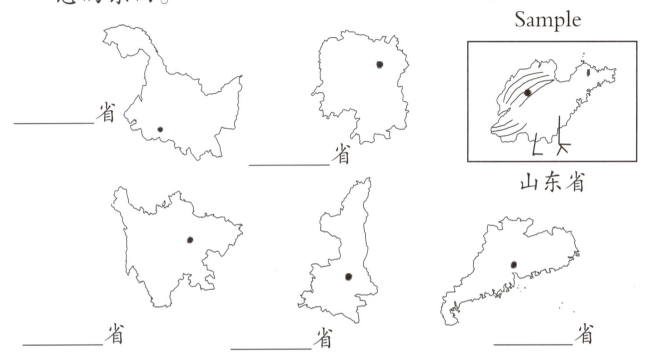

五　在下面的地图上找出上面你刚画的几个省，并涂色

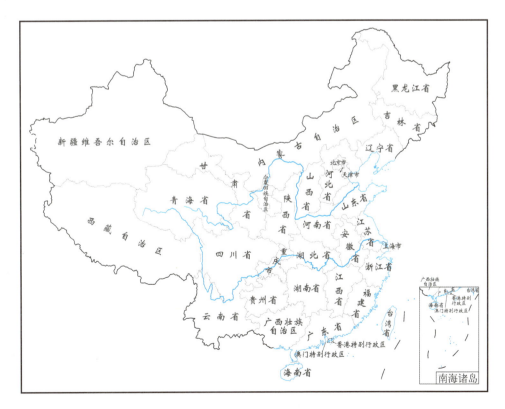

第十一课 中国名山（选修课）

★ 练习一　　　☆ 练习二　　　☆ 练习三

一　写生词

泰	山

朝	拜

石	刻

书	法

艺	术

二　组词

仙_____　　泰_____　　艺_____　　奇_____

刻_____　　拜_____　　黄_____　　客_____

三　写出风景区所在的省/自治区，然后涂色

涂色	风景区	省/自治区
🟦	泰山	
🟨	黄山	
🟩	桂林	

22

第十一课 中国名山(选修课)

练习一　**练习二**　练习三

一　写生词

风	景		

旅	游		

山	峰		

倒	影		

仙	境		

甲			

桂	林		

浮			

迎	客	松	

二　选择填空

1. 泰山在_____省，海拔_____。

　　（山东　山西　陕西）（4,510米　1,545米）

2. 泰山有几百处古代_____和2,000多处古人的_____。

　　（修建　建筑）（石刻　时刻）

3. 黄山之美，在于有_____、_____、_____、_____。（奇松　怪石　云海　温泉　倒影）

4. 人们都说"桂林山水_____"。

　　（家天下　甲天下　申天下）

第十一课 中国名山（选修课）

练习一　练习二　**练习三**

一　给"日"字只加一笔，变成另一个字，看看你能变出几个字

日　日　日　日　日

　　日　日　日　日

二　连线

- 黄山
- 泰山
- 桂林

第十一课 中国名山（选修课）

练习一　　练习二　　★ 练习三

三　根据《泰山石刻》选择填空

1. 秦始皇统一中国后，丞相李斯把这件功德写下来，刻在_____上。（黄山　泰山）

2. 两千多年来，许多_____、_____、名人都在泰山留下了自己的书法作品。

（士兵　农夫　帝王　书法家）

3. 风景秀丽的泰山，也是石刻书法艺术的_____。

（旅店　　博物馆）

四　熟读课文《中国名山》三遍

第一课　听写

1.	2.	3.	4.
5.	6.	7.	8.
9.	10.	11.	12.

第三课　听写

1.	2.	3.	4.
5.	6.	7.	8.
9.	10.	11.	12.

第五课　听写

1.	2.	3.	4.
5.	6.	7.	8.
9.	10.	11.	12.

第七课　听写

1.	2.	3.	4.
5.	6.	7.	8.
9.	10.	11.	12.

第九课　听写

1.	2.	3.	4.
5.	6.	7.	8.
9.	10.	11.	12.

第十一课　听写

1.	2.	3.	4.
5.	6.	7.	8.
9.	10.	11.	12.

1.	2.	3.	4.
5.	6.	7.	8.
9.	10.	11.	12.

1.	2.	3.	4.
5.	6.	7.	8.
9.	10.	11.	12.

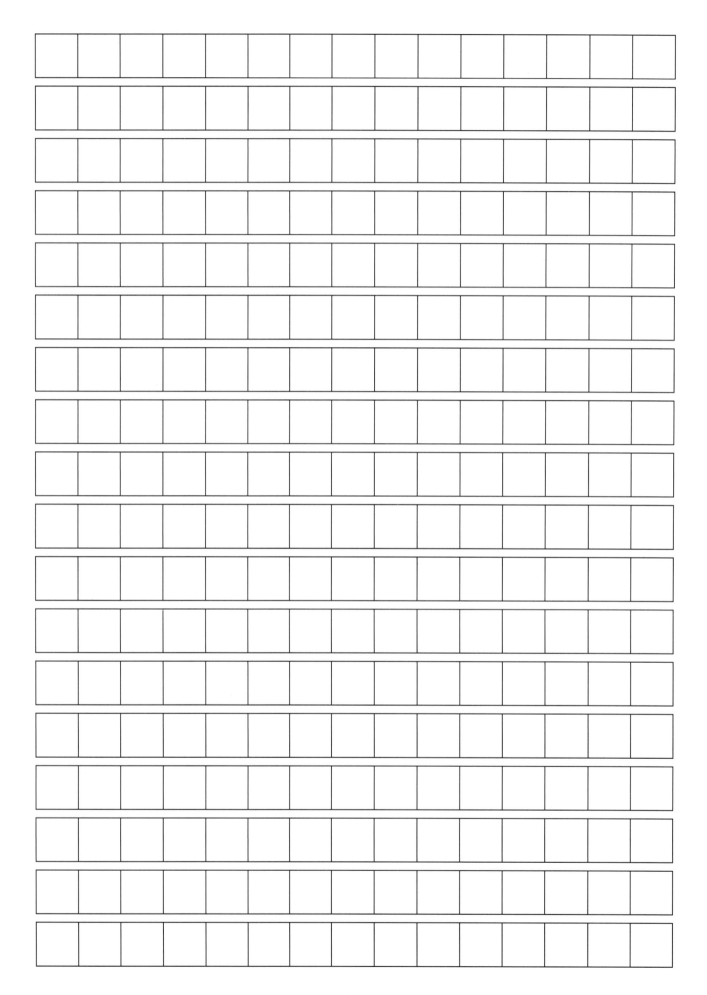

新双双中文教材 7
New Chinese Language and Culture Course

中国地理常识 Common Chinese Geography Textbook

练习本 双课

石雪丽 编著

北京大学出版社
PEKING UNIVERSITY PRESS

NanHai
BRIDGING EAST & WEST

目　录

第二课　　人口和民族 …………………………………… 1

第四课　　平原和盆地 …………………………………… 5

第六课　　气候 …………………………………………… 9

第八课　　野生动植物 …………………………………… 13

第十课　　著名城市 ……………………………………… 17

第十二课　名胜古迹（选修课）………………………… 22

第二课 人口和民族

练习一   练习二   练习三

一 写生词

人	口		

民	族		

亿			
占			

世	界		

分	布		

平	均		

二 组词

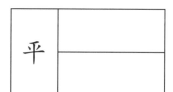

三 转换数字和中文

中文	数字
十四亿	1,400,000,000
	300,000,000
一万	10,000
八十万	
百分之十九	
	90%

四 上网搜索再填写

1. 你居住的城市有多少人口？_____

2. 你居住的国家有多个民族吗？他们是_____，_____，_____，人口最多的民族是_____。

第二课 人口和民族

练习一　**练习二**　练习三

一　写生词

居	住		

汉	族		

藏	族		

其	他		

地	区		

寿	命		

维	吾	尔	族			

免	费		

二　填空，并给图表涂色

中国有_____人口，占世界人口的19%，是世界上人口最_____的国家。

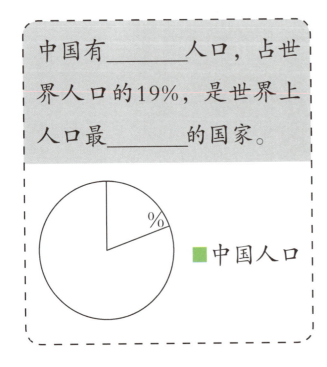

中国人口分布不_____，90%的人居住在_____。

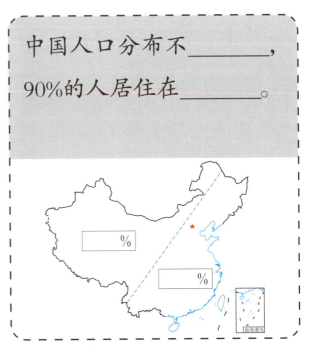

第二课 人口和民族

练习一　练习二　**练习三**

一　填空，再给图表涂色

中国共有_____个民族。其中____族人口最多，占91%。

■ 汉族
■ 少数民族

____%

少数民族主要居住在中国的西南、_____和_____地区。（按地区涂色）

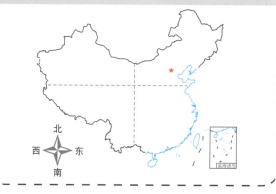

二　读一读，用画线的词语造句

我们游泳队的平均年龄为12岁。

平均_____。

三　这是哪些少数民族，请连线

蒙古族　　满族　　维吾尔族　　藏族

第二课 人口和民族

练习三

四 阅读《民族节日》，了解丰富多彩的民族风情

1. 连线

那达慕·　　　　　　　　　　·回族

开斋节·　　　　　　　　　　·傣族

泼水节·　　　　　　　　　　·蒙古族

2. 那达慕大会的主要活动有什么？画 ☑

☐骑马　　☐射箭　　☐摔跤　　☐赛龙船

3. 到了泼水节，人们会做什么？画 ☑

☐泼水　　☐骑马　　☐赛龙船　　☐唱歌、跳舞

五 朗读课文三遍，你记住了几个少数民族？写下来

第四课 平原和盆地

练习一　　练习二　　练习三

一　写生词

盆	地
肥	沃
天	津
浙	江
稠	密

| 经 | 济 | | | |

| 发 | 达 | | | |

二　组词

肥	
经	
达	
盆	

三　选择填空

1. 中国的平原主要分布在_____，占全国面积的____。

　　　　　　　　　（东部　西部）（90%　19%）

2. 长江中下游平原是中国的_____。

　　　　　　　　　　　　（最大沙漠　鱼米之乡）

3. 中国的四大盆地都在_____（东部　西部）。

第四课 平原和盆地

练习一　　练习二　　练习三

一　写生词

降	水	通	道	气	候	湿	润	农	业	内

二　选字组词

气（候　猴）　　（农　衣）业　　（稠　绸）密　　时（候　后）

经（济　齐）　　（盆　盘）地　　（把　肥）沃　　发（远　达）

三　给中国地势的三级阶梯涂色（从高到低 橙－黄－绿）

地形	所属阶梯
柴达木盆地	
塔里木盆地	
四川盆地	
华北平原	
东北平原	
长江中下游平原	三

第四课 平原和盆地

练习一　练习二　**练习三**

一　看课本第92页地图，填出三大平原、四大盆地名称

❶＿＿＿盆地＿　❷＿＿＿＿＿＿　❸＿＿＿＿＿＿　❹＿＿＿＿＿＿

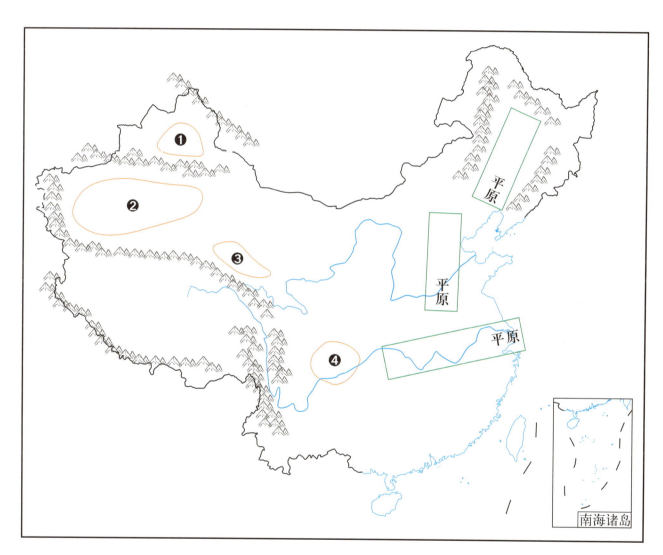

二　朗读课文三遍，记下你每次用了多长时间

1. ＿＿＿＿＿　2. ＿＿＿＿＿　3. ＿＿＿＿＿

第四课 平原和盆地

练习一　练习二　**练习三**

三　读一读，用画线的词语造句

上海的经济很<u>发达</u>。

发达＿＿＿＿＿＿＿＿＿＿＿＿＿＿＿＿＿＿＿＿＿＿＿。

四　根据《最长的沙漠公路》选择填空

1. 最长的沙漠公路穿过＿＿＿＿＿＿＿。

（塔里木盆地　四川盆地）

2. 这条沙漠公路两旁有＿＿＿＿＿＿＿。

（水井和植物　雪山和湖泊）

3. 这条沙漠公路全长＿＿＿＿。（525米　525千米）

五　根据《万丈盐桥》选择填空

1. 万丈盐桥在＿＿＿＿＿＿＿。

（塔里木盆地　柴达木盆地）

2. 盐桥将＿＿＿＿＿＿＿分成两半。（察尔汗盐湖　沙漠）

六　回答问题

你觉得人们为什么用盐铺桥，不用钢铁或者木头？铺成这座桥的那么多盐是从哪里来的呢？（可以上网搜索后回答）

＿＿＿＿＿＿＿＿＿＿＿＿＿＿＿＿＿＿＿＿＿＿＿＿＿＿＿

＿＿＿＿＿＿＿＿＿＿＿＿＿＿＿＿＿＿＿＿＿＿＿＿＿＿＿

第六课 气候

★ 练习一　　☆ 练习二　　☆ 练习三

一　写生词

复	杂

特	点

季	风

普	遍

影	响

二　组词

复	
季	
影	
普	

三　在图上填写主要气候类型，并按照要求涂色

气候类型	涂色
季风气候	绿
大陆性气候	黄
高寒气候	橙

第六课 气候

练习一 ★练习二 练习三

一 写生词

炎	热

因	此

降	雨

集	中

温	差

干	燥

纬	度

法	国

属	于

二 选字组词

干（燥 澡）　（纬 伟）度　（炎 淡）热　寒（令 冷）

影（向 响）　（诗 特）点　（李 季）风　气（温 湿）

三 写出反义词

　　　复杂——　　　　　　寒冷——　　　　　　干燥——

第六课 气候

练习一　练习二　**练习三**

一　读一读，用画线的词语造句

1. 中国气候<u>复杂</u>多样。

   复杂＿＿＿＿＿＿＿＿＿＿＿＿＿＿＿＿＿＿＿。

2. 夏季，中国<u>普遍</u>炎热。

   普遍＿＿＿＿＿＿＿＿＿＿＿＿＿＿＿＿＿＿＿。

3. 中国领土广阔，地势高低不同，<u>因此</u>气候多样。

   因此＿＿＿＿＿＿＿＿＿＿＿＿＿＿＿＿＿＿＿。

二　选词填空

> 农业　纬度　寒冷　炎热　干燥　大陆

1. 冬季冷风从＿＿＿＿吹向海洋。

2. 北部大陆性气候的冬季＿＿＿＿＿＿。

3. 夏季，中国普遍＿＿＿＿。

4. 季风性气候的高温和雨水同时到来，对＿＿＿＿非常有利。

5. 中国的齐齐哈尔市与法国巴黎＿＿＿＿相近。

第六课 气候

练习一　练习二　**练习三**

三　你居住的城市气候是怎样的，填空

1. 我住的城市纬度是_____，和中国的_____纬度相近。（城市）

2. 我这里最热是_____月，最冷是_____月，最冷时江湖_____。（结冰　不结冰）

四　根据《秦岭——中国南北分界线》选择填空

1. 秦岭位于中国_____。（中部　南部）

2. 秦岭南边比北边_____，是中国南北分界线。

（冷　热）

3. 很多著名的_____发生在秦岭。（历史故事　冷空气）

4. 用荧光笔（High lighter）画出秦岭—淮河的位置

第八课 野生动植物

★ 练习一　　　☆ 练习二　　　☆ 练习三

一　写生词

条	件

陕	西

甘	肃

体	态

秀	丽

二　组词

条_____　　川_____　　体_____　　顶_____

陕_____　　甘_____　　丽_____　　珍_____

三　选择填空

1. 中国自然条件_____。（复习　复杂）

2. 大熊猫生长在四川、陕西和甘肃的山区_____中。

（竹林　草原）

3. 黑龙江省有_____和_____。

（丹顶鹤　金丝猴　东北虎）

4. 丹顶鹤是一种名贵的鹤，被称为_____。

（神仙　仙鹤）

5. 白鳍豚是淡水鲸，生活在_____中。（大海　长江）

第八课 野生动植物

练习一 **练习二** 练习三

一　写生词

丹	顶	鹤

鲸

灰	白

贵	州

珍	稀

二　用1—2句话，说说每张照片里都有什么，有哪些珍稀动物

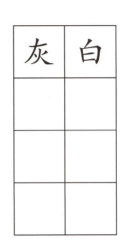
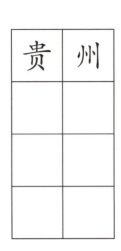

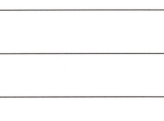

第八课 野生动植物

练习一　练习二　★练习三

一　写生词

水	杉

银	杏

珍	贵

药	材

二　根据《银杏树——"活化石"》选择填空

1. 银杏树可以活_____。（300年　3,000年）

2. 银杏树也叫_____。（公孙树　子孙树）

3. 银杏树的果实叫_____，可以吃。（白果　红果）

4. _____ 是银杏树的叶子。

　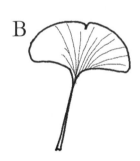　

A　　　　　　B　　　　　　C

三　朗读课文三遍，你觉得最难读的是哪句话？

第八课 野生动植物

练习一　　练习二　　**练习三**

四 找一找，涂一涂

- 在地图上找到这些地名
- 按要求把每种动物的的产地画上图案/颜色

（如：大熊猫的家乡是甘肃、陕西、四川，把这三省涂成浅绿色）

	珍稀动物	产地	图案/颜色
1	大熊猫	甘肃　陕西　四川	绿色
2	东北虎	黑龙江	黄色
3	丹顶鹤	黑龙江	圆点
4	金丝猴	四川　云南　贵州	斜线

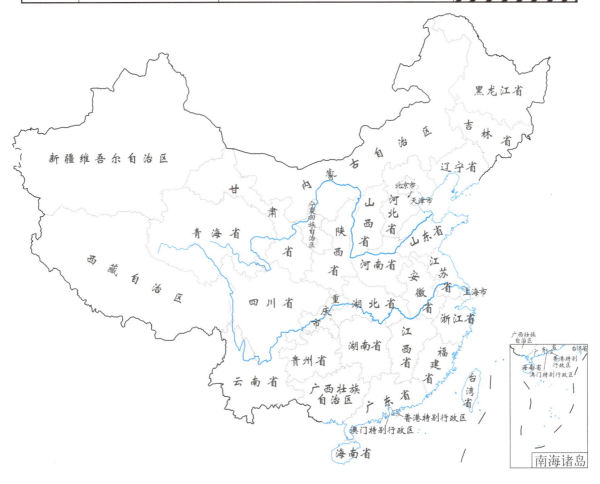

第十课 著名城市

练习一

一 写生词

现	代	化

朝

宫	殿

皇	宫

壮	观

名	胜	古	迹				

二 组词

城_____　　迹_____　　著_____　　观_____

修_____　　宫_____　　盘_____　　朝_____

三 读一读，用画线的词语造句

1. 故宫是一个大建筑群，十分壮观。

　　壮观_____。

2. 北京有许多名胜古迹，最著名是长城、故宫。

　　著名_____。

第十课 著名城市

练习一 ★练习二 ☆练习三

一 写生词

棋	盘

建	筑

沿	用

菜

二 选择填空

1. 中国的首都是_____。（北京　西安　上海）

2. 12世纪后，_____朝、_____朝和_____朝都定都北京。（汉　元　明　清）

3. 北京著名的名胜古迹有_____、_____、_____、_____。（长城　天坛　故宫　兵马俑　颐和园）

4. 故宫很大，有_____间房子。一排排高大的宫殿都是_____墙_____瓦。（9,999.5　1,000）（红　黄　灰　黑　绿）

5. 北京是中国的文化中心，有著名的_____和_____。（北京大学　清华大学　天津大学）

三 朗读课文《北京》三遍

第十课 著名城市

练习一　　★ 练习二　　练习三

四　作文：阅读课本第67页，介绍一个城市

要求：1. 突出城市特色　　2. 写作有条理　　3. 详略得当

第十课 著名城市

练习一　练习二　**练习三**

一　写生词

交	通	发	展	银	行	金	融	公	司	贸	易

工	厂	剧	院	商	店	旅	馆	餐	厅	繁	华

二　选择填空

1. 上海位于_____入海处，_____方便。

（长江　黄河）（交通　遍布）

2. 今日的上海是个_____大都市。

（博物馆　现代化　住宅区）

3. _____是中国最大的海港。（北京　上海　西安）

第十课 著名城市

练习一　　练习二　　**练习三**

三　看地图回答下面的问题

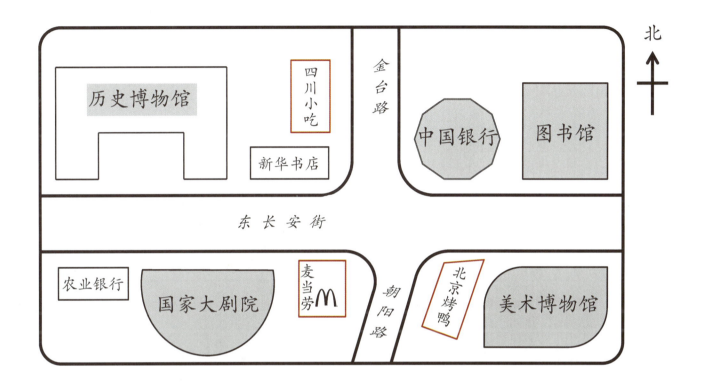

1. 地图中有_____家银行，_____座博物馆，_____家餐厅。

2. 离美术博物馆最近的餐厅是_____。

3. 从历史博物馆到国家大剧院要穿过哪条街？_____

4. 中国银行东面的建筑是什么？_____

第十二课 名胜古迹（选修课）

★ 练习一　　☆ 练习二　　☆ 练习三

一　写生词

| 烟 | | | | 军 | 事 | | | 敌 | 人 | | | 传 | 递 | | | 消 | 息 |

| 烽 | 火 | 台 | | | | | 电 | 报 | | |

二　选择填空

1. 长城建于2,000多年前，是古代的_____。

（军事工程　皇宫）

2. 长城东起河北的_____，西到甘肃的_____。

（嘉峪关　山海关）

3. 长城全长_____，也叫万里长城。

（6,700多千米　670多千米）

三　上网搜索后填写

6,700千米，相当于从你家到_____。

（地名）

第十二课 名胜古迹（选修课）

练习一　**练习二**　练习三

一　写生词

| 表 | 情 | | |

| 沉 | 稳 | | |

| 零 | 件 | | |

| 陵 | | | |

| 铜 | | | |

二　选字组词

表（清　情）　　（峰　烽）火台　　（消　清）息　　零（件　牛）

电（报　抱）　　（祖　组）成　　传（第　递）　　兵马（桶　俑）

三　根据课文和《有趣的兵俑》选词填空

　　秦始皇　表情　骑兵　西安　将军

1. 1974年，在中国_____发现了2,000多年前_____陵中的兵马俑。

2. 兵俑的_____有的认真，有的沉稳，真是千人千面。

3. _____俑共出土9件，他们是指挥官。

4. _____俑一手牵马，一手拿弓。

第十二课
名胜古迹（选修课）

练习一　　　练习二　　　**练习三**

千人千面的兵马俑

一　这是哪个人？从上图找出他的编号。

二　这15个头像中，哪个是将军俑？_____
　　　　　　　　　　　　　　　　　（编号）

第十二课
名胜古迹（选修课）

练习一　　练习二　　**练习三**

三　兵马俑的脸像不像一个汉字的形状？把人脸和汉字连线。据说，每个人都能找到一个和自己长得像的兵马俑

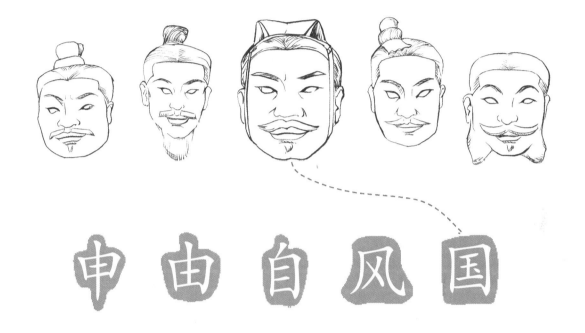

四　长城、兵马俑、泰山、黄山、桂林，请你选两个以上景区，从北京或上海出发，做一个全家的旅行计划，上网搜索交通、门票和住宿费用。请家长协助，参考网站：

携程 http://www.ctrip.com/　　去哪儿网 http://www.qunar.com/

时间	景点	交通 （飞机/火车/汽车，价钱）	门票	旅馆 （名字、费用）
第一天				

第二课　听写

1.	2.	3.	4.
5.	6.	7.	8.
9.	10.	11.	12.

第四课　听写

1.	2.	3.	4.
5.	6.	7.	8.
9.	10.	11.	12.

第六课　听写

1.	2.	3.	4.
5.	6.	7.	8.
9.	10.	11.	12.

第八课　听写

1.	2.	3.	4.
5.	6.	7.	8.
9.	10.	11.	12.

第十课　听写

1.	2.	3.	4.
5.	6.	7.	8.
9.	10.	11.	12.

第十二课　听写

1.	2.	3.	4.
5.	6.	7.	8.
9.	10.	11.	12.

1.	2.	3.	4.
5.	6.	7.	8.
9.	10.	11.	12.

1.	2.	3.	4.
5.	6.	7.	8.
9.	10.	11.	12.

中国地理常识 附加手工作业

设计：石雪丽

《中国地理常识》附加手工作业说明

学地理，一定离不开记地名。怎么让这些陌生的地名变得亲切呢？这一系列手工作业通过动手剪、贴、找和搜索，把地理知识立体化、生活化，使学生在学中文的同时，又获得了地理知识，真是一箭双雕。

这四个作业既可以配合"新双双中文教材"《中国地理常识》的教学内容，也可以单独使用。请老师根据进度布置作业，给学生2-4周时间完成。右表定周班建议进度。每课一周，每5课复习一次，考试一次。

每个作业的说明和样本在练习本里；每个作业完成后，用硬卡纸做，学期结束可以订成一本纪念册，送给学生，非常有保留价值。

讲课内容	手工作业	设计意图
第一课 亚洲最大的国家		
第二课 人口和民族	（一）民族小纸人	了解少数民族，多民族的中华文化更精彩
第三课 山地和高原		
第四课 平原和盆地		
第五课 江河与湖海	（二）立体地形图	地名形象化、立体化（需要提供3D foam adhesive squares）
一一五课 复习		
一一五课 考试		
第六课 气候		
第七课 农作物和名产	（三）美食地图	发掘自己身边的地理知识，走到学生身边
第八课 野生动植物		
第九课 行政区划	（四）家谱	追溯血缘关系，和地名建立亲切感
第十课 著名城市	填图封皮	
六一十课 复习		
六一十课 考试		

小制作（一）：民族小纸人

手工作业用纸第1页

请你参考网站"56个民族全家福"（摄影师陈海汶作品）http://slide.news.sina.com.cn/c/slide_1_435_9600.html 你喜欢哪个民族的衣服？用彩笔、彩纸、花布、毛线等做出2个民族小纸人来（画出来也可以）。小人儿可以是男的，也可以是女的；可以拿着东西，也可以做别的动作。请写出你做的小人儿是哪个民族。

样本：

小制作（二）：立体地形图

手工作业用纸第2、3页

1. 涂色，剪开

   中国地势像三级阶梯，从高到低，分别涂上：
   - 橘红色
   - 黄色
   - 绿色

2. 粘贴，泡沫双面胶（foam squares，是一种有厚度的双面胶，Crafts Stores 有，需要老师提供）

3. 在地形图上，用蓝色 marker 描出：
   长江　黄河

4. 把下面名称剪下来，贴在地形图上：

   ✂-------------------------------------
青 藏 高 原		四川盆地
黄 土 高 原	华 北 平 原	
云 贵 高 原	准 噶 尔 盆 地	
内 蒙 古 高 原	柴 达 木 盆 地	青海湖
长江中下游平原		鄱阳湖
塔 里 木 盆 地		洞庭湖
   ✂-------------------------------------

样本：

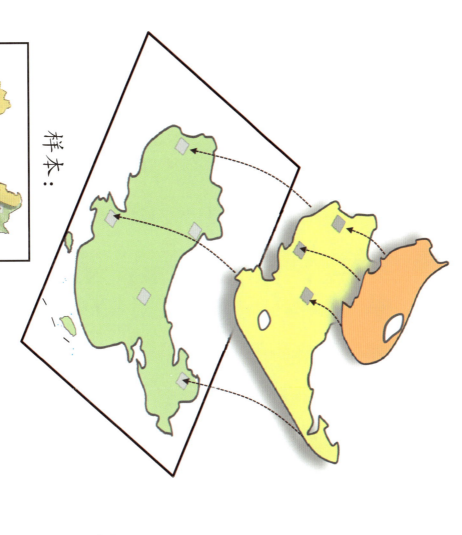

小制作（三）：中华美食地图

手工作业用纸第4、5、6页

你家的餐桌上，柜子里有多少中国地名？请家长带着孩子们在厨房里找找带有中国地名的食品标签。

- 剪下来，给它们编上号（比如：❶ 镇江香醋，❷ 绍兴料酒，❸ 青岛啤酒，❹ 新竹米粉……）

- 在地图上找找有它们的产地在哪里，把号码贴在手工作业第4页的空白地图上。

这个作业目的一定让学生多看地图，一定让中文书上的知识走到孩子们身边。等到学习第九课《行政区划》的时候，很多地名就不陌生了。

样本：

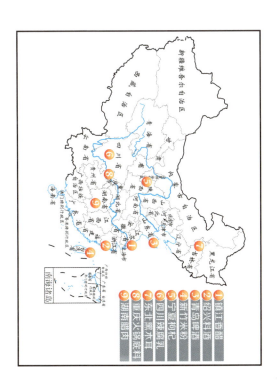

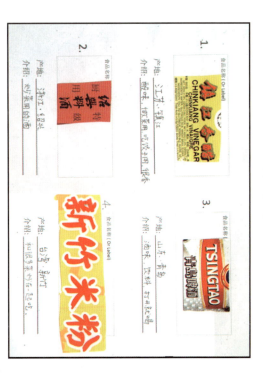

小制作（四）：家谱

手工作业用纸第7、8页

家谱就像是一棵家族树（Family Tree）。我们的先人一直在中国这块土地上生活，他们生活在什么地方？过得怎样？这些和你有着千丝万缕的联系。请父母或其他长辈帮助你完成下面两部分内容：

一、四代家族树

样本：

四代就是四个Generations. 包括：

1. 你的八位曾祖父母（Great-grandparents）
2. 你的四位祖父母（Grandparents）
3. 你的父母亲
4. 你自己和你的兄弟姐妹

请写出每个人的姓名和故乡（省、市或县），最好有照片，海外出生者写出生地国名，城市名。

二、传记

听父母讲一讲你的曾祖父母的故事，为你的一位曾祖父（母）写一篇简短的传记（Biography），至少包括关于他（她）的四个话题：

1. 出生时间、地点，请说明地理位置 *
2. 职业
3. 家庭情况：婚姻，子女，与你的血缘关系
4. 他（她）做过的哪件事或哪一个决定，最终影响了你父母来到海外定居？

样本：

* 地理位置：写出地形或山川名称，南方、北方、海边……

例句：
我的曾祖父□□□1908年出生在四川盆地的绵阳市……

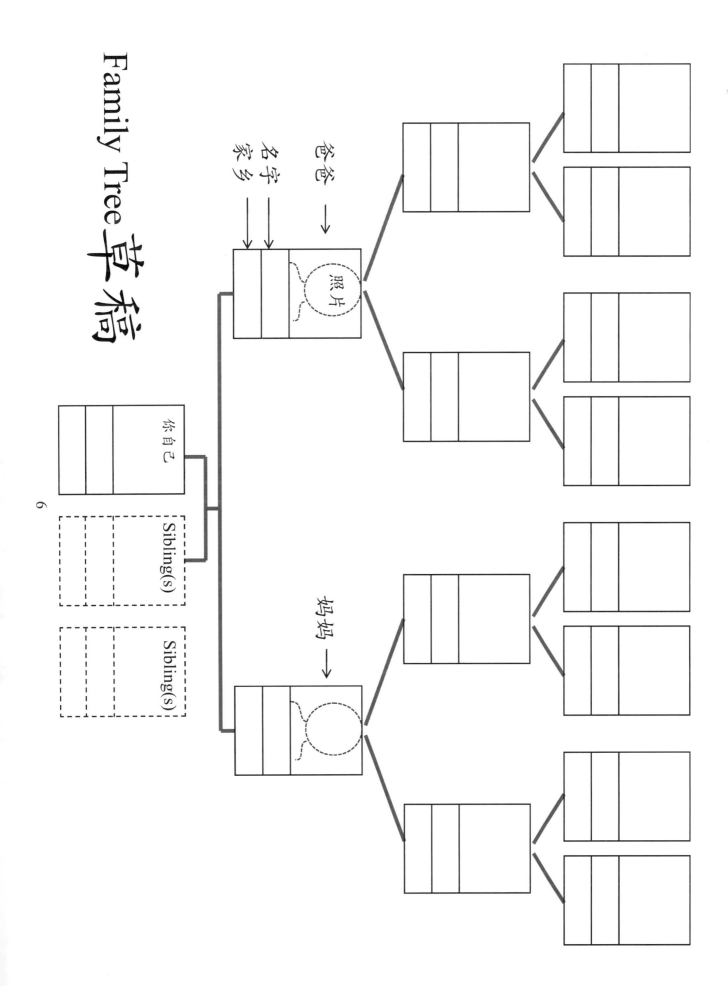

小制作：地理纪念册封皮

手工作业用纸省页

填写手工作业省页的行政区划地图并涂颜色。这是地理手工作业纪念册的封皮。

特别要求：填写整齐，可以美化，特别要突出你父母家乡的省或市。

样本：

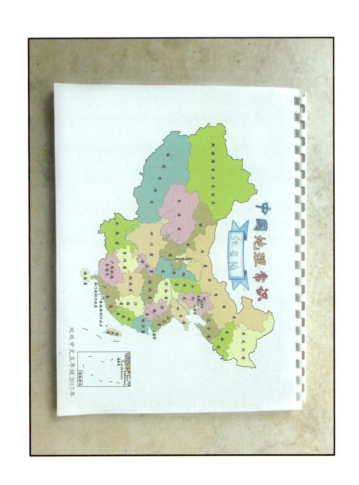

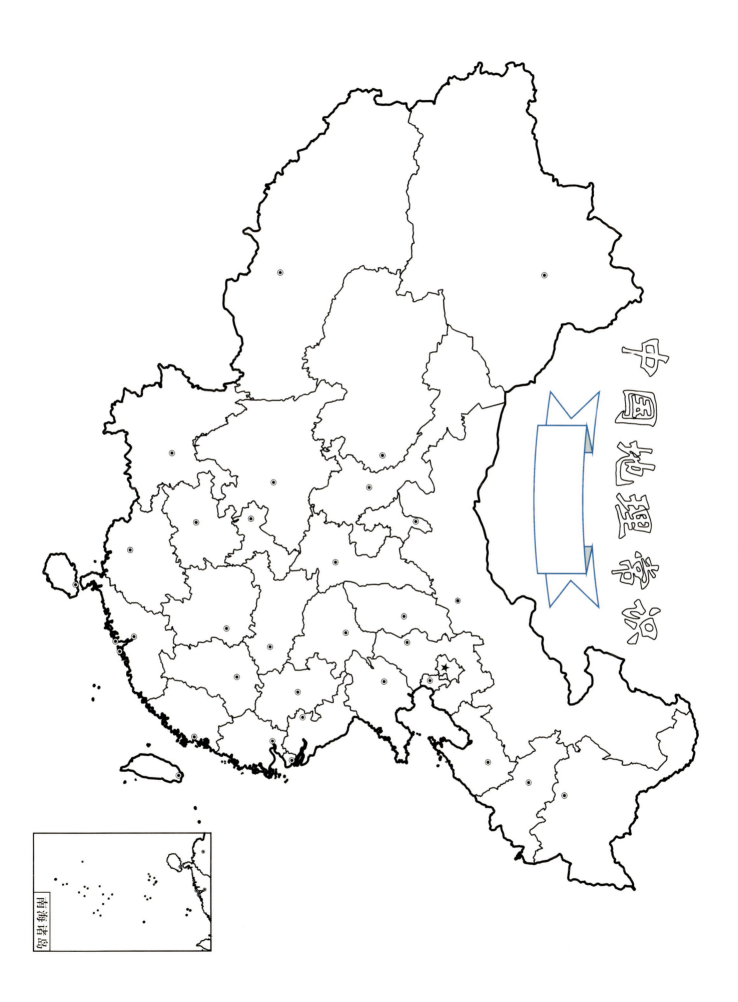

美丽的中国少数民族服饰

_____族

_____族

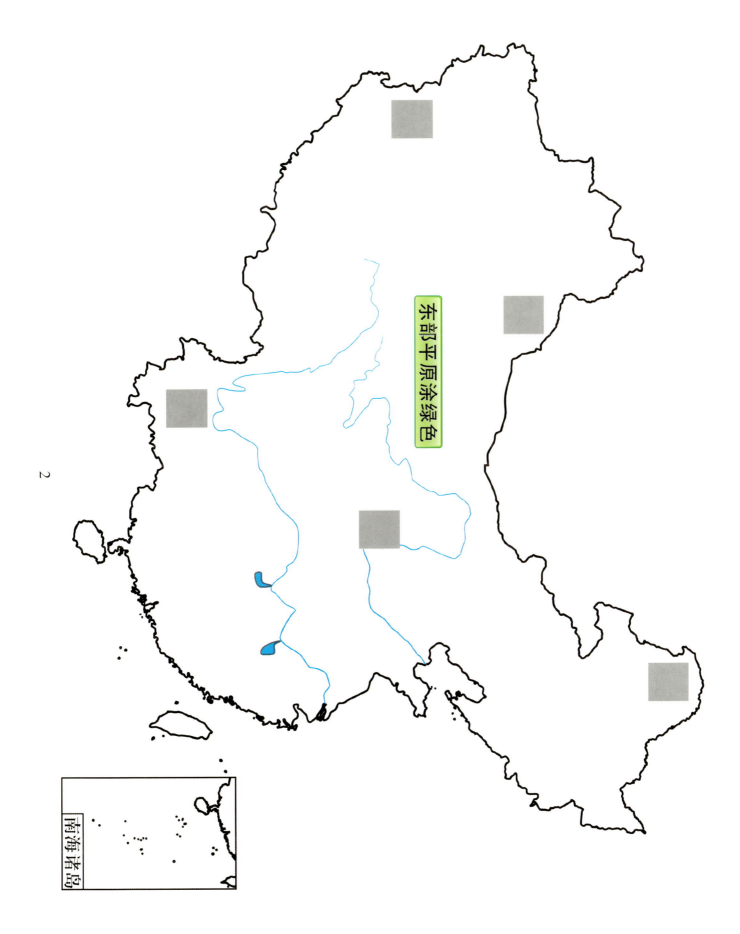

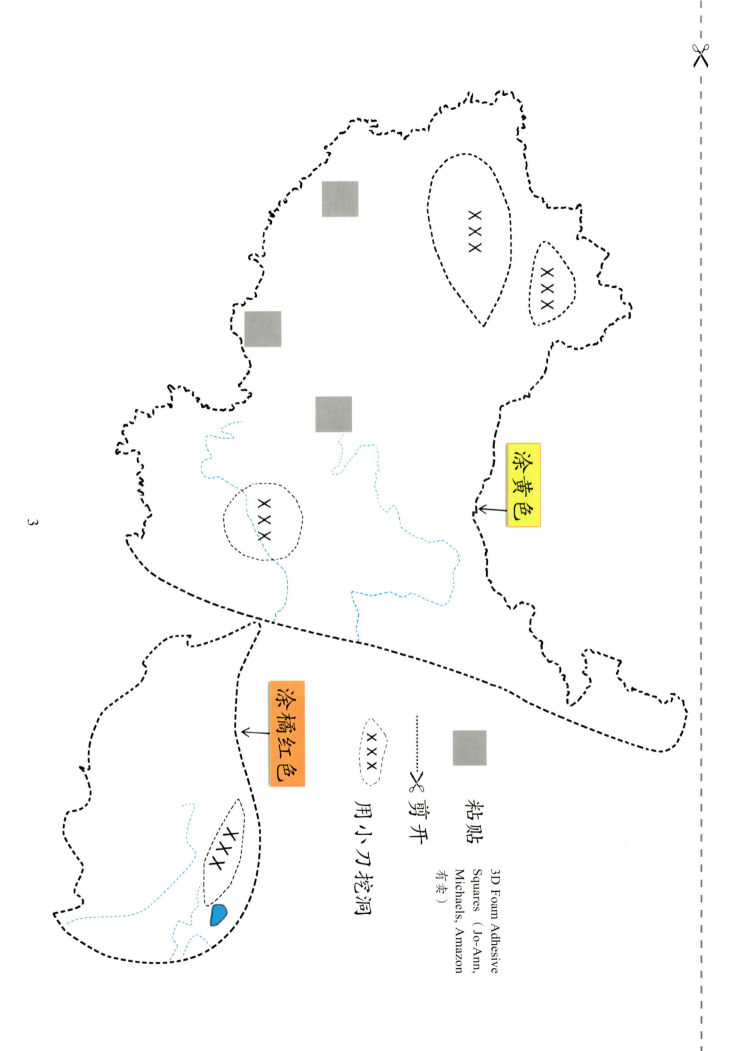

1	
2	
3	
4	
5	
6	
7	
8	
9	
10	
11	
12	

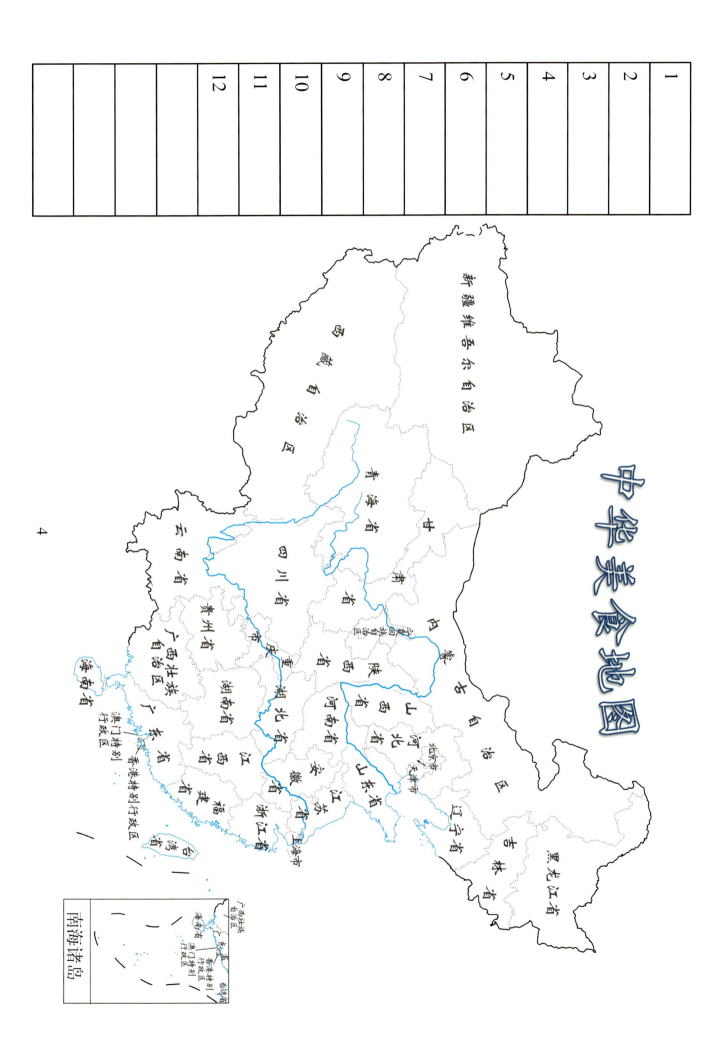

食品名称（Label）

产地：

介绍：

食品名称（Label）

产地：

介绍：

食品名称（Label）

产地：

介绍：

食品名称（Label）

产地：

介绍：

食品名称（Label）

产　地：_____

介　绍：_____

食品名称（Label）

产　地：_____

介　绍：_____

食品名称（Label）

产　地：_____

介　绍：_____

食品名称（Label）

产　地：_____

介　绍：_____

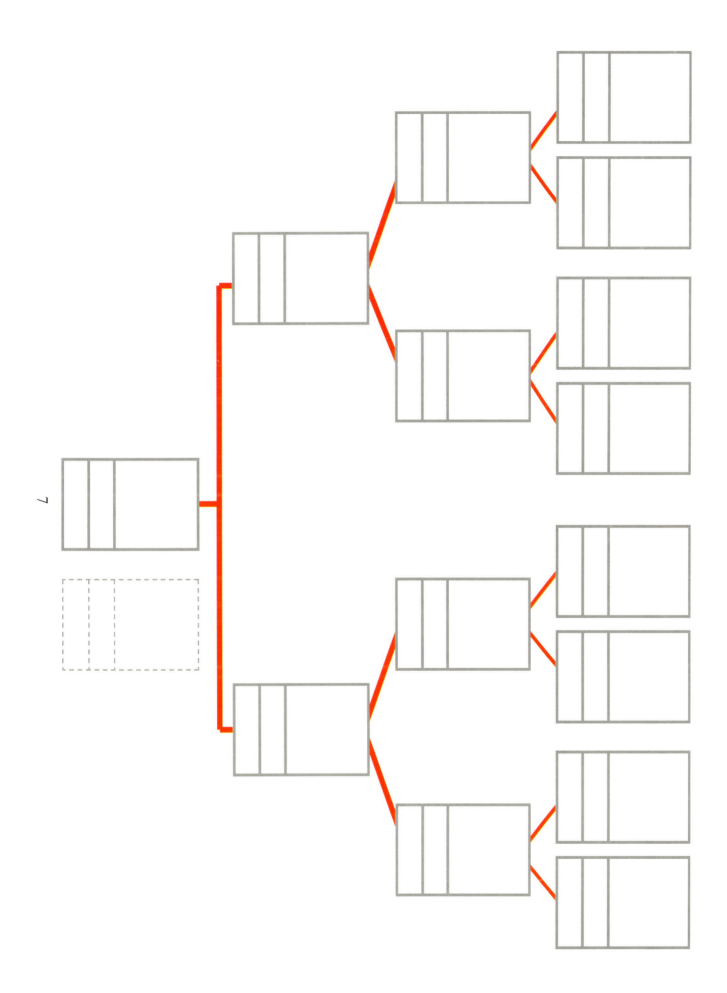

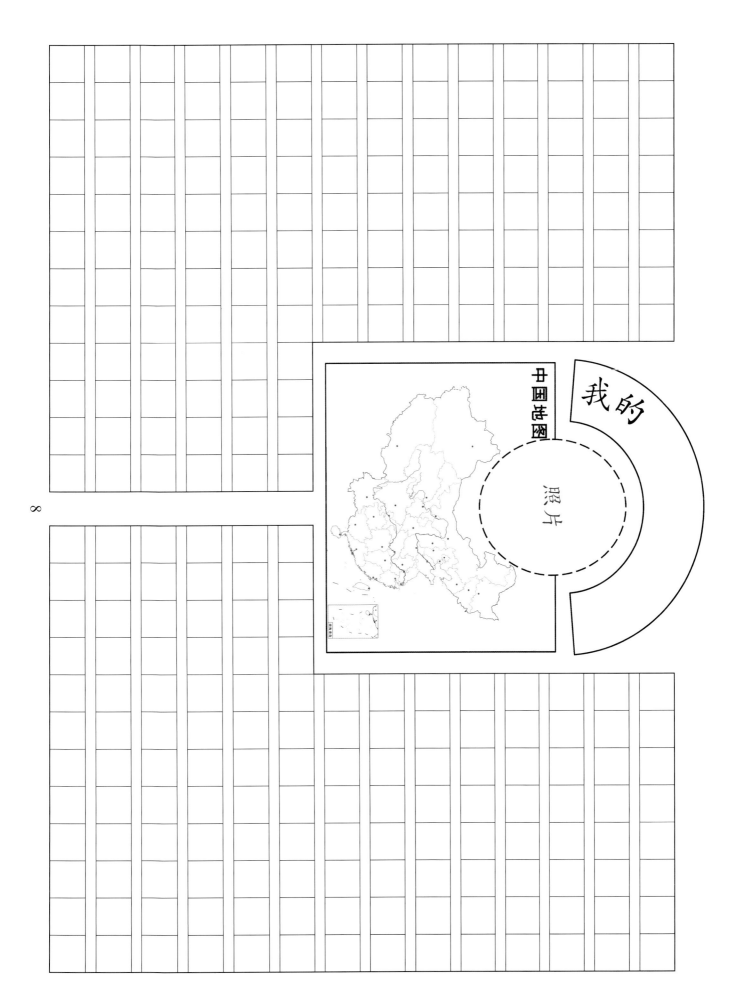